Lose the
business plan

Lose the business plan

What they don't teach you about being an entrepreneur

Allon Raiz

BOOK**STORM** MACMILLAN

ISBN: 978-1-920434-03-8

First edition, first impression 2010
Second impression 2013

Published jointly by Bookstorm (Pty) Limited and
Pan Macmillan (Pty) Limited

Bookstorm (Pty) Limited
PO Box 4532
Northcliff
2115
South Africa

Pan Macmillan (Pty) Limited
Private Bag X19
Northlands
2116
South Africa

Distributed by Pan Macmillan
via Booksite Afrika

Edited by Pat Botes
Cover design by Karin Barry
Typeset by Lebone Publishing Services, Cape Town
Printed by Ultra Litho (Pty) Limited, Johannesburg

Acknowledgements

Writing a book while building a business is not possible without help. This book is the result of many efforts. I would, firstly, like to thank all my Partner Raizcorp companies which provided me with the opportunity to learn. People believe that my role is to inspire and motivate my partners; the truth is, they inspire and motivate me. To be part of their journey and to observe how they persevere through their obstacles is incredibly humbling.

To those I mentor, thank you for your stories, for your wisdom, and for your trust in me.

To my partner at Raizcorp, Colin Kapeluschnik, thank you for your patience. This seemed to be a never-ending project. Finally, it is complete.

To my mentor, who would be mortified if his name were mentioned as he does not like the limelight, thank you for your guidance and your motivation but, mostly, thank you for the generosity in sharing your wisdom.

To my wife, for listening to me battle through chapter by chapter, thank you for reading and commenting and asking the important questions.

And finally to Trevor Waller, who worked tirelessly with me to write this book, thank you for the debates, the attention to detail and your incredible way with words.

To my sons, Cannen and Denim, build your sandcastles the way you think is best.

Contents

For the sake of convenience, the word 'he' has been used throughout to mean 'he or she'. No sexist implication is intended.

I know not what I appear to the world, but to myself I seem to have been only like a boy playing on the sea-shore

Sir Isaac Newton

Boy meets mentor

I have lost count of how many business plans have crossed my desk. I stopped reading them a long time ago. Almost every business plan I have ever read lacks the one ingredient that ultimately determines the success of the business – and that is the entrepreneur. The most crucial component of a small business seems to be the one thing that gets overlooked by banks, funders and government institutions looking to grow small businesses.

One man taught me this lesson. He taught it to me by giving me a chance. He never asked me for a business plan. He, a dollar billionaire, looked at a 25-year-old who had nothing and said, 'You choose the business; I'll invest in it'. What I heard was, 'I'll invest in you'. My mentor asked me about my life, my experiences, my thoughts. He listened carefully – beyond the words and the fears. He looked carefully – beyond the youth and the bravado that accompanies it. He looked and he decided that I had 'it' – the entrepreneurial heart – the heart to persevere, to carry on no matter how hard it gets.

And so I started a business. And it failed. And I started another one. And it succeeded. And through all the travails, my mentor never gave up on me. He knew that I was an entrepreneur. He understood that entrepreneurs don't give up. They often want to, but they persevere. They push through and they continue to build their business.

I built a few businesses – some succeeded; others didn't. Building them interested me more than running them. And, with this realisation, I found my passion. I began supporting entrepreneurs and soon realised there was a business opportunity in growing entrepreneurs and making their businesses profitable. The vehicle that I use to do this is called Raizcorp. Raizcorp is what is known as a business incubator. It partners with selected small businesses and supports the entrepreneurs to enable them to grow. Entry into Raizcorp is difficult; we apply a long and intense selection process. But not once during the entire process do we ask for a business plan.

We know that business plans are rarely written by the entrepreneurs themselves; indeed, business plan writing is one of the fastest-growing industries! Often written by third parties, most business plans – whatever the business or the entrepreneur – look the same. The finance sections are particularly interesting. If business plans are to be believed, all small businesses follow the same trajectory. With their finances looking like a 'J-curve', all small businesses should be hugely profitable by their third year. In 20 years of working with entrepreneurs, I am yet to see a business whose path closely follows the predictions of their business plan.

There is, of course, a problem of logic here which we need to examine: Banks only provide finance to entrepreneurs on the basis of business plans, and yet 96% of small businesses fail. Something is going wrong. The evaluation of whether a business will succeed or not – based on this document we call a 'business plan' – is faulty. The business world is too fluid for entrepreneurs to be married to their business plans. Among other things, it is resilience, and the ability to adapt to changed circumstances, that will determine the business's success. The numbers presented in a business plan often bear no resemblance to reality and are of little value if the entrepreneur himself has not thoroughly thought through his business. And this, essentially, is the point: The thinking process that creates the business plan is what counts – not the actual document. If an entrepreneur is to succeed, he needs to understand and own the thinking behind his business, on every level. The thinking that goes into the creation of the content of the plan is what counts. And the person doing the thinking needs to be the person who will be building the business. That person is the entrepreneur.

Like a map, a business plan is just a representation of reality. I understand the need for business plans. But I maintain that the value of the business plan lies in the process of crafting it, not in the finished document.

Rather than focusing on the business plan, banks and investors need to be looking for what my mentor looked for in me. They need to look for entrepreneurs who have the drive, the fight and, most importantly, the ability to tolerate the pain and uncertainty that accompany the choice to be an entrepreneur and build a business. They need to look for entrepreneurs whose willingness to take calculated risks is as great as their desire to build their businesses.

I believe unequivocally that the principle of backing the jockey (i.e. the entrepreneur) and not the horse (i.e. the business) is the best way to ensure entrepreneurial success. And so my team and I work tirelessly to identify the entrepreneurs who have what

I call the 'blue heart' of the entrepreneur. This book is written for those entrepreneurs – the entrepreneurs who want more than just being able to work for themselves. They want to build a business and grow it beyond themselves. These are the entrepreneurs whom I support and with whom I am blessed to work. In this book, I will share with you some of the things I have learned on my own journey as an entrepreneur and in my work supporting entrepreneurs.

When entrepreneurs join Raizcorp, we have them sign an entrepreneurial oath. I offer it here, by way of introduction, as it encapsulates my understanding of the entrepreneurial choice.

> *I have undertaken a journey of growth and pain. I understand that there will be many dark days where I will want to throw in the towel, but won't. I know that, for what might seem the longest time, I will dread month-end. I am comfortable with being pressured by my family and friends to get a real job. I am prepared to lie awake, for many nights, planning my way out of perceived imminent failure. I am ready to be told by my potential clients that I am too expensive or too inexperienced. I anticipate falling so many times that I will ache as I stand up again.*
>
> *For I know that it will all be worth it in the end as I extinguish the words of my naysayers and the loudest of them all – the one that lives in my head.*
>
> *For I am an entrepreneur; I have chosen this life above immediate comfort as I strive to create wealth and to make a difference in the world around me.*

One of the key debates, in which I often find myself participating, is whether entrepreneurship can be taught or not. Can you learn how to be an entrepreneur from a book? I have a library full of books – *Ten Steps to Wealth; Eight Paths to Entrepreneurial Nirvana* ... the list of promises goes on. More than anything, these books have taught me that entrepreneurial success has got very little to do with technical know-how. Successful entrepreneurs have an attitude that is almost impossible to teach. They have an attitude towards risk, coupled with a desire to build, that differentiates the winners from the also-rans. This book seeks to reveal some of these softer determinants of success – all the while being cognisant of the fact that there is no formula. This book is about the ingredients; it will not give you a recipe. The recipe, I am afraid, will always be up to you.

The statistics tell us that 96% of all small businesses fold within ten years. The statistics are frightening; they say 'get a job'. I say 'don't'. The economy needs small businesses and it needs big entrepreneurs. What it does not need is bigger business plans. By all means, think through your business, plan it carefully, and raise the money, if that's what you need. But then, lose the plan. Do the work and read the signs; adapt and build. Keep going.

Through my work, and through this book, I aim to play my small part in turning these statistics on their head. I hope that you will learn a lot and, more than that, I trust that it will give you the courage to stay the course. The entrepreneurial choice is a difficult one. I believe it is worth it. Trust your choice, trust the process and enjoy the journey!

PART 1

Are you an entrepreneur?

Doers, dreamers and saints

If I told you I was a doctor, or a lawyer, or even a teacher, you would probably have some idea of what my job involved. But what if I tell you that I'm an entrepreneur? What mental image will form in your head? The chances are that my telling you that I'm an entrepreneur will not tell you much about what I actually do. There really is no universally accepted definition or understanding of what exactly constitutes this journey we call 'entrepreneurship'.

Having chosen to dedicate my life to growing entrepreneurs, I am constantly on the lookout for new definitions and ways of understanding what it means to be an entrepreneur. Over time, I have found more than 500 definitions of what an entrepreneur is and does! I think it is safe, therefore, to say with confidence that all entrepreneurs have three major things in common: They see an opportunity, take a risk and, in so doing, create value.

I once found this description of an entrepreneur: 'a determined, decisive, dedicated doer and dreamer'.[i] That's quite a list of attributes. And, recently, I came across the following response to an article on entrepreneurship:

> *This article seems to state that being an entrepreneur is all about receiving some sort of financial gain. What about the likes of Mother*

Teresa? Is she considered to be an entrepreneur? I do think so and yet she did it for the compassion and commitment she holds – not for any monetary reward.

And so I Googled 'Mother Teresa + Entrepreneur' and, lo and behold, came across an article entitled 'Mother Teresa: My Marketing Hero', which went on to describe Mother Teresa as 'one of the greatest entrepreneurial marketing geniuses the world has ever known'.[ii]

Now, all these writers may very well be correct. I am not arguing for, or against, any of their ideas or definitions of entrepreneurship. But, it seems to me that the word 'entrepreneur' has become a catch-all term for all kinds of people in business. I don't want to add to the confusion about what characterises an entrepreneur. But, because this book is about entrepreneurship, it's important that I make it clear right at the outset that, when I use the word 'entrepreneur', I am referring to a specific type of entrepreneur, i.e. the growth entrepreneur. Before I expand on this, I want to state that I am not in the business of judging others – there is space enough for all kinds of businesspeople and entrepreneurs. I am not judging the choices people make when they go into business. I am, however, suggesting that not all people who start their own businesses are growth entrepreneurs. It took me many years to work out that I was indeed a growth entrepreneur. Now that I know, I believe that, before you choose to undertake a business endeavour, it helps to know what type of entrepreneur you are, or want to be.

Essentially, there are three types of entrepreneurs:

■ **Subsistence entrepreneur**. These entrepreneurs own, and generally are, their own one-man band businesses. The business has no real value in that it relies completely on the entrepreneur and generally does not make consistent profits.

■ **Lifestyle entrepreneur**. Like the subsistence entrepreneur's business, the lifestyle entrepreneur's business also has no substantial value in that it cannot be sold without the entrepreneur. However, the lifestyle entrepreneur's business does make consistent profits, and the profits are sufficient to sustain the entrepreneur's lifestyle.

■ **Growth entrepreneur**. This entrepreneur's business does have value and relies decreasingly on the entrepreneur. It may, or may not, be making profit but it has the potential – without the entrepreneur – to generate profit.

Each of these entrepreneurs is important in an economy; each is equally valid. But, when I talk about entrepreneurs, I am talking about growth entrepreneurs. Let's look more closely at the differences between lifestyle and growth entrepreneurs.

Lawyers, plumbers and other lifestyle entrepreneurs

A lifestyle entrepreneur is the traditional one-man band, or even a member of a small three- to five-person operation. Many lawyers and plumbers are good examples of lifestyle entrepreneurs. If my lawyer or plumber is ill or chooses to go on holiday, he is unavailable to provide me with a service and cannot, therefore, receive income. I recently returned a gas canister to my local hardware store. The owner advised me to leave my empty canister and come back in two weeks' time to fetch a new one. 'I'm going overseas for a family wedding,' he explained, 'and the shop will be closed while I'm away.' This man owns and runs a shop but the fact that his shop cannot exist without him makes him a lifestyle entrepreneur. What this means is that he aims to use his own knowledge and expertise to offer the best possible value to his clients. He offers value to his customers in terms of service and convenience. But, without him, there is no service or convenience; without him, the shop is closed!

The wealth-creation strategy of lifestyle entrepreneurs is to increase their revenue by increasing their own value to the client. A good example of this is the family doctor who becomes a specialist. By investing in further education, the doctor may improve his skills and become a surgeon. He can then charge much more for his services. This does not, however, make the surgeon a growth entrepreneur – it makes him a highly skilled professional in his own business. Without him, there is still no business!

Although to many people the hardware store owner may seem more like an entrepreneur than the surgeon, both have an equally valid claim to entrepreneurship – after all they both run a business! By my definition, growth entrepreneurs build businesses beyond themselves. Neither the hardware store owner nor the surgeon can go on leave without closing their business down. And this, for me, is the litmus test. When the surgeon invests in a practice, takes on partners and hires staff, he begins to move away from a lifestyle to a growth orientation.

Where does the value lie?

When Raizcorp first started, I was it; Raizcorp was me and my dream. To grow, I had to bring in new partner companies: businesses that Raizcorp could incubate. In persuading these companies to join, I was essentially selling myself – what I, Allon, could offer them. After all, I was the business; the business was me.

By the time the thirtieth new partner company came on board, Raizcorp had grown too large for me to be personally involved in the intake process. I no longer take part in the recruitment of potential Raizcorp partners. The process is handled by other role-players at Raizcorp. I often don't meet the company owners until all the paperwork is signed and sealed. Raizcorp is no longer Allon Raiz. I have removed myself almost completely from the function of recruiting partner companies.

The fact that new people can join Raizcorp, and that I am not involved in the process, fills me with excitement. For many entrepreneurs, the prospect of making themselves 'redundant' in the processes of their own business is a scary thought. Many entrepreneurs are control freaks. But, like the hardware store owner, holding on too tightly keeps the business small. When we let go of the reins, we allow the horse to pick up speed.

At first, Raizcorp's partner companies were buying into me as a person. I offered them my knowledge and experience in the hope that they would buy into my vision. At that time, Raizcorp's 'value proposition', i.e. the tangible results to a partner company of using the services of Raizcorp, lay entirely within Allon Raiz. A business's value proposition answers the questions: 'What makes you different?' and 'What value will you deliver to your clients?' In the early years of most businesses the value proposition lies wholly within the entrepreneur. Raizcorp's growth is the result of a gradual process in which its value proposition has moved from lying within me to a place where it now lies within the business. And that is the secret to growing a business.

The difference between being a lifestyle entrepreneur and being a growth entrepreneur lies squarely within understanding the concept of value proposition. When you are a lifestyle entrepreneur, the value proposition lies within you. When you are a growth entrepreneur, the value proposition lies within the business. By growing the value proposition of your business, you move from being a self-employed one-man band towards becoming a business run by an entrepreneur who focuses on growing the business's value proposition. As you grow the business, you make it increasingly attractive to customers or clients, thereby generating the profits needed to employ people who, in turn, should also increase the business's value proposition. It is an endless, but vital, loop to success.

Today, the value proposition of Raizcorp lies in its ability to offer its partner companies an infrastructure, personnel, training, mentoring, coaching, sales, and a community of like-minded people. The value proposition has moved far beyond the individual who began the business.

Different strategies

When I train people, I use these diagrams to help explain the concept of value proposition and how to shift the value proposition from the individual (entrepreneur) to the business.

Diagram 1: The business is the individual; the value proposition to the client lies in this person; the individual provides a service and the client pays for it.

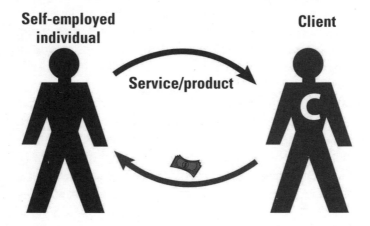

Diagram 2: Although the entrepreneur has grown his business, he remains the link between the client and the business. The value to the client lies within both the entrepreneur and the systems he has set up in the business. The client pays the entrepreneur who then uses the money to continue building value-creating systems.

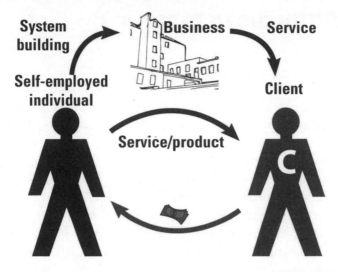

Diagram 3: The business systems are sufficiently established so that the entrepreneur no longer needs to be an integral part of the value loop. The client pays the business for the services he receives, which are independent of the entrepreneur's input. The business provides value, the client provides the business with payment, and the entrepreneur reaps a financial reward without being directly involved in the transaction. This reward may be in the form of a salary, dividends or profit share.

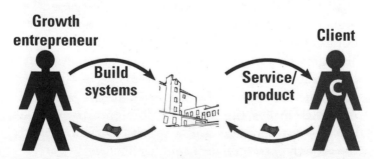

Attitudes to growth

I was explaining the difference between lifestyle and growth entrepreneurs to a graphic designer who has had his own business for a few years. He challenged my view: 'My clients don't pay me,' he said. 'They pay my company.' I then asked him if anyone, besides himself, created value for his clients. Since he is the only person employed by his company, the answer was, of course, no. He, like many lifestyle entrepreneurs has fooled himself into believing that, because he has created a company that actually receives the money, it is his business that provides the value. But, without any transfer of the value beyond his own skills, the graphic designer is not growing his business in any way. He is merely working harder and stressing more. After all, a day off is a day with no income! That's not growth, that's self-employment!

It is this attitude to growth that differentiates the two types of entrepreneurs. When growth entrepreneurs start out, they hold the value proposition of the business in their hands, just like the lifestyle entrepreneur does. But growth entrepreneurs employ a very different strategy from that of lifestyle entrepreneurs. The growth entrepreneur puts in place systems, processes and products so that, over time, he transfers the value proposition from himself to the business. And therein lies the essential difference between a lifestyle entrepreneur and a growth entrepreneur – the growth entrepreneur is not his business!

Growth entrepreneurs transfer as much value as possible into service or physical products and processes in order to extract more value and volume from their customers. At some point, the entrepreneur's own personal value is no longer important to the delivery of value to the customer. The value lies in the business, not within the entrepreneur.

I want to make it very clear that I am not saying that growth entrepreneurs are 'better' than lifestyle entrepreneurs; nor am I advocating for one side or the other. I make the distinction to clarify a widely used term that happens to be the topic of this book and the passion of my life. But, most importantly, I make the distinction to assist the would-be businessperson. Understanding whether you are a lifestyle or growth entrepreneur will predetermine the strategy you choose on your way to success and wealth. The hardware store owner I mentioned earlier may truly be wondering why he is not making the money he dreams about. And, if he asked me for advice, I would point to his loyal assistant – a young, articulate and bright man who, while the owner was away, could quite easily have run the store. But, the owner is not thinking like a growth entrepreneur – he has not taken any steps to transfer the value proposition from himself to his business.

It is this attitude to growth that differentiates the lifestyle entrepreneur from the growth entrepreneur. The hardware store owner's thinking is probably characterised by one or more of the following thoughts:

■ 'I don't trust him; he might steal from me.'

■ 'No one else can do the job as well as I can.'

- 'What if he does the job better than I do?'
- 'I don't want this thing to get too big for me to handle.'

These are the thoughts of a lifestyle entrepreneur. The growth entrepreneur replaces each of these thoughts with an *action* designed to grow his business:

- Instead of 'I don't trust him; he might steal from me', the growth entrepreneur says, 'I put in place the controls that allow me to track inventory and prevent theft'.

- Rather than thinking, 'No one else can do the job as well as I can', the growth entrepreneur thinks, 'I train my employees and provide them with the templates, standards and benchmarks that enable them to perform as well, if not better, than I can'.

- While the lifestyle entrepreneur worries, 'What if he does the job better than I do?', the growth entrepreneur states, 'I surround myself with people who are better than I am precisely because that is the key to growing my business'.

- And, finally, rather than fearing, 'I don't want this thing to get too big for me to handle', the growth entrepreneur is confident: 'Trying to do everything myself will limit my business. I put in place the right managers and processes to be able to handle growing my business'.

So, decide what you want to be – a lifestyle entrepreneur or a growth entrepreneur – and employ a strategy appropriate to that choice.

If you wish to be a lifestyle entrepreneur and stay that way, I wish you luck, wealth and prosperity. And, although this book is geared at growth entrepreneurs, I trust that you too will find much value in it. Perhaps you are a growth entrepreneur – and don't yet know it! If you wish to be a growth entrepreneur, this book will give you advice, tools and strategies to grow your business to a point where *you* are no longer the critical success factor in order for the business to serve its market!

One of the many differences between being an employee and being an entrepreneur is that employees get to go home. They can leave their work behind. Entrepreneurs do not have that luxury. And, while many books will tell you how important it is to find 'balance', this is not one of those books. This book is about learning how to be an entrepreneur.

You will learn that being an entrepreneur is not a job – it is a state of mind. Based purely on my own experiences of living entrepreneurially, I will offer suggestions on how to be entrepreneurial in your every action and thought.

Conventional wisdom states that the successful entrepreneur must exhibit specific characteristics, such as tenacity and focus – the implication being that the tenacious and focused individual is somehow better equipped to be an entrepreneur. This is by no means a certainty. Focus can lead to closed-mindedness. Tenacity can become obstinacy and the inability to change. This book will show you that all human characteristics are potential strengths or weaknesses in an entrepreneur. It is *self-awareness* that ultimately determines the likelihood of your success. I would rather support an entrepreneur who is aware of his potential to become distracted than the single-minded individual who is unaware of his potential inflexibility.

So, in my experience, self-awareness is the key. What exactly do I mean by 'self-awareness'? In the next section, we will look at the 'ingredients' for success. We will examine what you need to know about yourself in order to become a successful entrepreneur.

PART 2

Creating success

Same ingredients:
different combinations

There is no single formula for entrepreneurial success. I have worked with many entrepreneurs and seen many different paths to success. Each of us is an individual with different experiences, values and outlooks on life. Given the same set of inputs, 100 entrepreneurs will have 100 different outputs. There are, however, certain 'stepping stones' on the entrepreneurial path that are common to most success stories.

While the stepping stones may be of different sizes, and even different distances from each other, they often follow a similar sequence. I believe that success, as an entrepreneur, is difficult without the following stepping stones:

In this section, we'll look at each of these stepping stones in detail.

Model: Stepping stones towards entrepreneurial success

Desire – 'It's my oxygen'

Ellen came to see me recently. She is a former nurse who now runs an HIV and Aids training company, which she founded. She is looking to grow her business. Within the first five minutes of our meeting, Ellen uttered the magic words, 'I love doing training. It's like oxygen to me – I can't live without it.' Ellen's words are the words of desire. She is telling me that she is doing what she enjoys. Many entrepreneurs fall into their business by accident. They end up doing something that is unconnected to their passion and then they wonder why their business is not working. When I meet entrepreneurs, I ask them a simple question: 'What would you like to be doing if you weren't doing this?' If they can give a quick answer to that question, they're doing the wrong thing! Their work is not their 'oxygen' – and, if you're going to be an entrepreneur and you really want to grow your business, it's going to need to be your oxygen for a while.

Very often, entrepreneurship is romanticised; the road to entrepreneurial wealth is glamorised. What these enthusiasts don't teach you is how hard it is. And, without desire you will struggle to make it. Desire is almost the inoculation against the downside. It is desire that gives you the ability to carry on when sales are down and you're not closing deals.

Unfortunately, I am yet to see a business plan with the heading 'desire'. Yet, without the deep desire to make your business successful, you will, at best, be an entrepreneur trapped in your own small business with intermittent successes and irregular pay. Your highs will be short-lived and your lows will be hell. Without deep desire, and passion for what you are doing, you might as well get a regular job.

Vision – 'I want it; I see it'

If desire is the *wanting* of success, vision is the *seeing* of success.

Successful people see their success long before they achieve it. This is what visualisation is. Jim Carrey, one of the highest paid comic actors in the world, sent his 'résumé' to the popular television programme of the 70s – 'The Carol Burnett Show' – when he was ten years old! Later, he wrote himself a cheque for a million dollars, which he looked at every day to keep himself motivated and focused on his goal. He imagined himself earning the money – and today he earns far more than a million dollars a film.

Visualisation is a very powerful tool. It has transformed many lives. One of my favourite descriptions of visualisation is the following:

> *The power of visualisation is energy – energy that allows you to enter the movie of your dream life enough times until that dream life finally becomes your actual physical reality.*[iii]

Our thoughts really do create our reality. There are many books and websites that discuss visualisation, if you want to find out more. My purpose here is for you to understand that entrepreneurial success requires you to picture your successes. On a daily basis, in the same way that the tennis player sees himself winning Wimbledon, you need to see your business growing;

you need to see the money coming in and you need to see yourself winning.

Vision is a much overused term. Corporates speak of their vision; government departments have visions. And, of course, every business plan begins with a section on 'vision'. Everybody, it seems, has a vision – printed and framed and stuck on their walls. This is not what I mean when I say that entrepreneurial success depends on vision. Vision, in the context of entrepreneurial success, means something very different to me. When I mentor entrepreneurs about their vision, the first thing I ask them to do is to distinguish between their own personal vision and the business's vision. I call these visions the difference between a cow and its milk.

Cow and milk vision

Some entrepreneurs focus on the milk, the by-product of the cow. But they forget to think about what they want their cow to look like. The cow is the business that generates the milk for the entrepreneur. Entrepreneurs need to understand what they want their cow to look like and they need to determine whether that cow will be able to generate the milk they desire. The entrepreneur who wants to live by the sea and drive a Porsche, but whose vision ('cow') is a small two-man business, is less likely to achieve his goal ('milk') than the entrepreneur whose vision is for his business to employ 100 people. In the latter's case, the cow has some hope of generating the quantity of milk that the entrepreneur needs to fulfil his personal vision. Some entrepreneurs are so busy focusing on

31

the milk that they don't think about what the cow (their business) needs to look like. In the meantime, their cow is still only a calf and they're waiting for it to supply gallons of milk! So when you visualise what you desire, you have to visualise both the cow and the milk and understand the relationship between the two.

Delusions versus visions

While it's vital to have a vision – something to aim for – your vision has to be realistically achievable. I'm not saying don't dream big. But set your short- to medium-term goals in such a way that you *will* be able to achieve them. Realism is often, unfortunately, one of the things missing in the business plan. Too much realistic thinking may not secure the loan! Sadly, it is the lack of realistic thinking that will sink the business. I was in conversation with the directors of a small three-man IT business when one of them told me that his vision is for them to be as big as Microsoft. Now, is that a vision or is it a delusion? I ask myself two questions that help me to distinguish between vision and delusion.

The first question is: Does the entrepreneur have some form of understanding of what it takes to achieve the vision? In talking to the entrepreneur, I try, in my mind's eye, to see if there is a dotted line of connectivity between the vision and where the entrepreneur is now. Along the way – from present reality to realisation of vision – there will be many boosters and boulders. But the entrepreneur has to have some way of articulating what it takes to get there. He needs to be able, even in the loosest way, to connect the dots between where he is now and his vision. And so I ask these directors what they think they need to do to become Microsoft. I listen carefully to their answers and, based on their inability to connect those dots, I don't think they're dealing with a realistic vision. They're dealing with a delusion and they need to bring their vision just a little closer to their reality. They cannot articulate, in any way, how they intend to move their small business out of their garage.

And so I ask the second question, which relates to the entrepreneur's trajectory: What are you doing now to move yourself towards your vision? Many entrepreneurs aren't taking the requisite actions to bring themselves closer to the realisation of their vision. Currently, these entrepreneurs have unhappy clients and, even at this stage of their business, they're not providing the services they promise. They're not doing the work – there is no indication that they are moving forward in the direction of their dream.

Vision without action is delusion. It's as simple as that.

The horizon of your vision

I doubt that Asa Griggs Candler, founder of the Coca-Cola Company, or Ray Kroc, founder of the McDonald's Corporation, had a vision when they started out of their products being sold in every country of the world. Their original goal would have been much less ambitious and more realistic. As their businesses grew, so too did their vision. A friend of mine, who built the largest Internet company in South Africa, once told me that, when he and his partners started out as students working from a small office on a university campus, their vision was to have twelve companies as their clients! So they set out to achieve that vision and, having followed the dotted line in pursuit of that vision, they allowed themselves to extend the horizon of their vision. And it is the relentless pursuit of the answer to the question 'How big can this get?' that is the driver of vision.

Desire asks: 'Do I want it?' Vision asks: 'How far can I push this?' But it is discipline that makes champions.

Discipline of motivation

I would love to run the New York City Marathon. The reality, however, is that right now all I have is the *potential* to run the marathon. No amount of wishing or hoping is going to prepare me for the race. Walking around my office every day will not prepare me, nor can I start training the day before the marathon. If I am to run, and finish, the marathon, I am going to need to embark on a daily training regimen and I'm going to need to stick to it. The *potential ability* to do something is not really worth anything if it is not accompanied by desire and, more importantly, discipline. Somehow, we find it easier to associate discipline with things that are related to our physical beings – gym and diets, for example. But success in business is no different from success in the New York City Marathon. Without discipline, you are as unprepared to succeed in your business as you are to run a marathon.

Entrepreneurs usually score well on the desire part of the equation. Many successful entrepreneurs are motivated to succeed. But motivation will only get them so far; eloquence and confidence will only be enough to get them started. Without discipline, it is very difficult to become a champion. Unfortunately, it is very hard to capture 'discipline' in a business plan. Yet, in the same way that great sports champions need discipline to be the best, the *entrepreneurial champion* also needs a very specific discipline – the discipline of motivation. Sportspeople have the discipline to remain motivated. They may stumble, they may fall, they may lose a race, but the champions get up because they are motivated to continue. Champions are the ones who are tough enough to stay on track; they keep their vision in mind and use it to keep pushing themselves further. As an entrepreneur, you will encounter obstacles everywhere, some of which will make you trip. The question is: Are you disciplined enough to remain motivated?

Cultivating good habits

There is really no secret to developing the discipline of motivation. Entrepreneurs need only look at what sports champions do to become the best – and do the same. The motivation and discipline of sportspeople is cultivated by daily habits, rituals and programmes, which have become a part of their life. To become an entrepreneurial champion, you also need to cultivate habits, rituals and programmes that motivate you and keep you motivated to succeed. You need to build routines into your life. You need to train yourself to focus on the positive, to magnify your successes, and to visualise even more successes. And then you need to keep doing it – every day, every week, every month – until it is integrated into your daily life. Success does not necessarily come easily. It requires hard work and dedication. But it also requires small steps. Start today and do it again tomorrow. That is how people get fit; that is how they succeed. Discipline is as much a requirement of entrepreneurial champions as it is a requirement of sports champions!

I have a daily, weekly and monthly routine, which I follow with unquestioning dedication.

At the beginning of every month, I write down my goals for the month. I write both my personal and business goals on specially printed pages inserted into my Filofax (yes, I still use one!). I then close my eyes and visualise each of my goals happening. In my mind's eye, I imagine the results of my goals becoming reality. When I achieve a goal, I record this on the flip side of 'my goals sheets' – 'my successes' sheet. I record each success, no matter how small, as an achievement to celebrate. Every morning before I shower, I review my goals and successes. When I step into the shower, I have my successes in my mind. I tell myself that I am achieving my goals.

'I may; I can; I will; I am'

To make sure that I am completely motivated when I leave my house to go to work in the morning, I've also built a routine into my morning shower time. I chose my shower time for this because it is something that I do every day. This is important for entrepreneurs. It's hard to create new habits. So it's better to find a way of integrating a new habit into an existing habit – something that you already do every day anyway.

In the shower, I begin by stretching and touching my toes. I choose stretching as it is a physical sensation that brings me to the present and forces me to concentrate.

As I stretch, I visualise my milk goals. Let's say, for example, that one of my goals is to grow Raizcorp to a $100-million business by the time I am 45. As I stretch, I say four different sentences for each goal. I call these my 'I may; I can; I will; I am' meditation:

■ I have the right to grow a $100-million business by the time I am 45. 'I **may**' communicates my right to achieve my goals – I tell myself that I have as much right as anybody else to achieve them.

■ I have the ability to grow a $100-million business by the time I am 45. 'I **can**' communicates that I have the ability to achieve my goals – when I say 'I can', I focus on what I need to do to achieve my goal.

■ I **will** grow a $100-million business by the time I am 45. 'I **will**' communicates that I have a strong intent to achieve my goal. But 'will' is not only about intent; it is also about having what it takes to achieve the goal. I stretch longer and harder and I then say to myself, 'I **have** the will' to grow a $100-million business by the time I'm 45. 'I **have** the will' expresses that I have what it takes to build a $100-million business by the time I'm 45.

■ And, finally, 'I **am**' when I stand up and visualise myself having achieved my desire. I play out the whole movie in my head. In the case of my financial goal, I see my bank statement and I visualise the bottom line – $100 million. I'm there – I have achieved it! I smile.

When I finish my shower, I once again picture having achieved my goal. And so, every morning, in my mind's eye, I have achieved my desires. When I step out of the shower, my motivation levels are high enough to deal with whatever comes my way that day. But, more importantly, I know why I am going to work each day; I know why I am facing fears and overcoming obstacles. My goals are clear and I am moving towards them – disciplined and motivated to achieve them.

Of course, if I stepped out of the shower every day and then sat and watched TV or went for a round of golf or met a friend for a long leisurely breakfast, my desire, vision, discipline and motivation would be wasted. Ultimately, it is action that separates the medallists from the 'also-rans'. Yet, so many entrepreneurs that I meet don't know this simple fact: Entrepreneurial success requires action. It is work, work and more work that results in success. The question is: Are you ready to start the climb to the top?

Discipline to act –
'That was my idea!'

Picture the scene: You're at a bar having a drink with a friend. Mounted on the wall is a television and, out of the corner of your eye, you spot a man receiving an award from the Minister of Trade & Industry. The award is for his exporting one million 'doofy jabs' to India. This particular 'doofy jab' has been patented and is a world-first. As the man steps up to receive his award, your friend elbows you, 'I came up with the idea for that "doofy jab" years ago,' he says bitterly, as he takes another sip of his drink.

Do you know someone like this? Are you, perhaps, that someone? The difference between the man in the bar and the winner of the award is quite simple really. The difference is *action*. The world is full of people who have great ideas; some of these ideas are even commercially viable. But an idea without action is just that – an idea. It is something that exists only in the mind. And something that exists only in your mind cannot, by its very nature, make you successful.

Many would-be entrepreneurs are stuck at the idea phase. I meet them on a daily basis. Over time, I have begun to sort them into types. There are the theorists, the perfectionists, the principled ones, those who are waiting and then there are the ones who are just plain lazy. None of them has yet found a way to put their ideas into action. Let's take a closer look at each of them.

The theorist

This type is a great researcher. He knows all the latest theories and, as a result, spends his time comparing his current situation to the published theories. And, when the theory and reality match, he'll begin taking action. That's when, in his mind, he'll be successful, when the world will finally sit up and notice him.

It's easy to recognise the theorist. He's the one using words like 'international best practice' and 'benchmarking'. He knows all the buzzwords and he's waiting for all the components of his idea to be in place before he makes a move. Unfortunately, the chances of *everything* being in place at the same time are negligible – and so the theorist never takes action. Someone else always gets there just before him ... and so he goes back to his research.

The perfectionist

For this type, nothing is ever good enough; it's always the wrong time, the wrong person, the wrong finance – something's always wrong. And he needs things to be 'just right'. In reality, this person is hiding behind the lie that he's a perfectionist; in reality, he's just fearful. But it's easier to hide behind the supposed flaws in the system or in the business. When confronted by this type, my standard line is 'Your product's good enough for market – just get it out!'

41

The principled entrepreneur

This type is married to his 'standards'; he spends his time seeking out the principles that provide him with the excuse not to take action. He uses phrases such as, 'I'd be compromising myself' or 'I would never do that'. This is the vegetarian who wants to open a restaurant but refuses to serve meat. Now, there's nothing wrong with being a vegetarian but, in a market of meat-eaters, where vegetarian restaurants are highly specialised and not very successful, this person needs to seriously question whether there wouldn't be a better way to make money than to open a restaurant! When confronted by these types, I very carefully try to steer them in other directions. The vegetarian is likely to have more success doing specialised catering or selling his products to retail outlets. Somehow, these would-be entrepreneurs always seem to find a standard or principle that gets in the way of their ability to take action!

The waiter

This type is waiting – for somebody else to do something, for something to happen, for a law to be passed, for re-zoning to take place, for the right person to come along. This waiter – eternally the victim of circumstances unrelated to his own actions – has an external locus of control. This means that the waiter does not believe that he controls his own destiny. And so the waiter finds it very hard to move beyond the wonderful idea that he feels is constantly being sabotaged by circumstances beyond his control.

The lazy one

Instead of looking within himself, this type will use every excuse in the book to explain away his lack of action. He is the one watching the afternoon soaps wondering why he's not making money! These people hide behind the need to have 'balance' in their lives to explain their long lunches and golf games. Somehow, they're always stressed because they're not making money. But, when I ask, I can see that they're not doing anything to make the money. My advice to them is simple: Do the work!

A gear called action

Action is truly the kingpin of success. I use the analogy of a car to explain how important action is. You can buy the most powerful and expensive car on the market; you can fit it with the best tyres; you can fill it with the best high-octane fuel; and then you can rev it all you like. But, until you engage the gears, your car is going to go nowhere. In business, taking action is like engaging the gears in a car. And without action, you and your business – no matter how good it may look on paper – are going nowhere. And so it is with entrepreneurs. It really doesn't matter how good your entrepreneurial qualities are – you have to engage that action gear.

All the types of entrepreneurs mentioned above have one thing in common – fear. If you dig deep enough, you will find that all entrepreneurs who are not 'in action' are held back by fear. And, for me, the opposite of fear is self-belief. The more you believe in yourself and your abilities, the less you fear and the fewer excuses you need to make. In order to gain self-belief, you need courage and self-insight.

I recently mentored a young entrepreneur named Katlego. He is a photographer who is slowly building a business based on his passion. Although the business is growing, it seemed to have plateaued and Katlego was stuck. In conversation he revealed to me that, in primary school, he had been the only black boy in his class. Although he was accepted and had friends, on some level he always felt like the outsider looking in – an observer, rather than a participant. This is, of course, a perfect position for a photographer; it was no surprise that he had been drawn to this profession! The problem was that Katlego had adopted the observer stance for all his life activities, not just photography. Katlego, despite his success, remained a scared little boy, not willing to fully risk getting involved. During a personal development course, Katlego made this connection between his boyhood experiences and his chosen career, as well as how he was keeping himself stuck. This realisation was huge for him. His decision to overcome this fear and to play 'flat out', to get involved and get his hands dirty, despite the fear, has shifted Katlego and is allowing him to grow his business beyond all expectations.

Like Katlego, many entrepreneurs need to change the way they think about themselves and the world in order to overcome their fears. They require a completely new paradigm. In the next section, I will share with you some tools that I recommend to entrepreneurs who wish to take action but are stuck in fear.

Stop comparing!

My wife had to give a talk for a well-known company. She is not a natural public speaker and spent weeks learning her speech by heart. When the time came to speak, she was a bundle of nerves and did a terrible job. The reason she messed up was not because she is a bad public speaker. She messed up because she was so busy trying to remember her speech and comparing what she was saying to what she had rehearsed, that she couldn't talk naturally. In her head she had a framework, and throughout her speech she was comparing her performance to the framework; when she digressed from the prepared speech, her mind-speak became, 'I made a mistake'. This is an example of a self-constructed standard to which my wife was comparing herself. The next time she had to speak, instead of a rehearsed and verbatim presentation, she prepared guidelines and so was able to stand up and speak from the heart – she had no comparison between a version in her head and the reality. I believe that losing the comparison is a very important tool for overcoming fear.

A business plan is another very good example where it is often necessary to 'lose the comparison' and not stick to a rigid framework. An entrepreneur may plan, for example, to sell 50 units by mid-year. When June rolls round and he has sold only 30 units, the panic sets in. And many entrepreneurs get stuck in the panic. My advice: Lose the comparison; deal with reality!

Be prepared for failure

According to some statistics, the average entrepreneur has 3.8 failures before he achieves success. I think this is nonsense – the average entrepreneur experiences 3.8 *million* failures before achieving success! In my experience, entrepreneurs are failing, on one level or another, on a daily basis. They fail to get orders; they fail to retain staff; they fail to get payment on time; they fail to make an impression at a networking event – the list goes on.

When you understand that your success is built on hundreds and thousands of both failures and successes, you stop taking the failures personally. You ride the waves and take the knocks. Failure becomes an expected part of your entrepreneurial choice and you no longer see failure in business as something that you need to take to heart. One of the secrets of coping with failure is to make sure that you have lots of options. Don't get blinded by the one big deal that may or may not happen. If you have only one big deal in the pipeline, then failure to close it could destroy your business. Entrepreneurs who tender for government work often forget to keep their options open. They are so busy filling in the myriad forms required by these tenders that they convince themselves that they will definitely be the preferred provider. They neglect their regular customers and forget to chase any other deals. When the tender does not go their way, they are devastated. I have seen entrepreneurs close their business after losing a tender!

Re-framing

In his book, *Yiddishe Kop* (literally 'Jewish Head'), Nilton Bonder writes about the way the Jewish people have used humour in the face of incredible hardships. He describes a technique called 're-framing' which has allowed the Jewish people, through the centuries, to find the good – or look for the humour – in even the direst of circumstances. Re-framing becomes a function of survival – it transforms a negative situation into something that can be viewed positively. I believe it is a valuable tool that entrepreneurs can use in order to survive. There is a hidden opportunity in every obstacle. What is required is the ability to re-frame it. Ironically, I learned this ability from my parents when they literally had to re-frame. My parents, who owned an umbrella factory, had received a huge order for umbrellas. They duly ordered the frames from their overseas supplier. To my parents' horror, while the frames were still on their way to South Africa, the order was cancelled. Facing insolvency, my parents asked a very simple question: 'What if this was a blessing?' And then they literally re-framed the umbrella frames. They suggested that the factory use the frames to create a whole new variety of umbrellas – different from the conventional umbrellas that were then available. They designed innovative umbrellas and hit the market with great success. So the deal that fell through became the basis for my parents' success. Instead of collapsing, my parents re-framed and turned a problem into an opportunity. It is a lesson I have often remembered when things haven't worked out quite the way I planned.

Unintended consequences

I recently discovered the Law of Unintended Consequences. Having lived and experienced it in its many forms, I was so surprised to discover that it was an actual law that I called a colleague at night to share my excitement. Parenting is a great mirror for this law. Good parents always try to act in the best interests of their children. But how do they know what the consequences of their actions will be? They simply don't. I think the secret is to embrace the law and to use it to your advantage. By knowing that there are always unintended consequences, you are able to accept life's unfolding events and to know that, even in the darkest moments, there will someday be an unintended consequence. Often, that consequence – with the benefit of hindsight – is a blessing. When I look back, there are so many dark moments the consequences of which became the blessings of my life. For example, my devastation when a seven-year relationship ended looked very different when I met my wife. So, as an entrepreneur, when the deal doesn't happen, the client doesn't show, or the tender goes to someone else, know that there may very well be an unintended consequence to the event. The consequence may be a lesson; it may be a hidden opportunity or a better deal. You simply do not know. So, while you rant and rave, and cry and scream, don't neglect the Law of Unintended Consequences – it will help you deal with the downturns that are an inevitable part of the entrepreneur's journey! With every unintended consequence comes the opportunity to re-frame.

Understand that it's all iterative

This is a particularly difficult lesson for the perfectionist type. 'Iteration' is a computer term that describes a constantly repeated operation or process – over and over, a program goes through a series of loops. Bill Gates understood the nature of iteration. When he launched the first version of Microsoft Word, it was not perfect. Once in use, a large number of 'bugs' became apparent. By getting feedback from users, the programmers could work on improving it. The second version was better but it still had bugs. And so it continued, with each subsequent version improving on the last. Microsoft Word is still far from perfect, yet it remains the dominant word processing program in the world.

Gates understands that the only way to get better is to take your product to market, get the market's feedback and then improve on the product. Every successful product and service goes through this series of loops on its path towards excellence. Because of the fickle nature of human beings, no product can ever be perfect; no product can be all things to all people. But each version of the product is an improvement on the previous version. You are far more likely to create a better product in the long run by taking the risk of the first step and getting your product to market than by sitting in your office, fearing the reaction should your product not please everyone. I doubt we would have cellphones or laptop computers if their creators were waiting for perfection!

Accept the down days

As much as I strongly believe that action is the key to success as an entrepreneur, I also recognise that there will be many days when you simply will not be able to find the energy or the will to take action. Be aware of this. On these days, it is important not to make rash or important decisions. Rather, wait for a new day with new opportunities. Occasionally allow yourself to be weak and inactive; accept that the down days are part of the process. The entrepreneurial journey is tough – accept the lows as much as you do the highs.

Filtering your actions

Many successful people attribute their success to simple *filters* (or rules, if you will) about making money. Some of these filters have almost become clichés.

Ray Kroc, founder of the McDonald's Corporation, used William Dillard's famous maxim 'Location, location, location' to turn McDonald's into the largest owner of prime real estate in the world!

Raymond Ackerman built his Pick 'n Pay empire using his simple philosophy of the four pillars of retail: consumer sovereignty, strong administration, the correct merchandise and social involvement. In an interview, he stated simply, 'Any activity that this enterprise involves itself in will be reflected in one of these areas'.

Kroc, Ackerman and many other successful business-people use simple filters like these to make their decisions. They base these filters on their values and philosophies. I'll go into this in more detail, but first, let's make sure that we have the same understanding of both these words – values and philosophies – that are commonly used though not always understood.

Philosophies and values

When I speak of a person's 'philosophy', I'm using the word to mean 'any personal belief about how to live or deal with a situation'. Of course, our personal philosophies are very closely connected to our values and, when I speak of 'values', I'm referring to a person or group's 'beliefs in which they have an emotional investment'.[iv] Your values will dictate whether you are for or against something. Believing that you should not have sex before marriage, or that you should respect your elders, are examples of different kinds of values that will inform your philosophy and dictate your actions in a given situation.

Many entrepreneurs begin well. They make some money and then, suddenly, they're back where they started. They've lost the money. And so they start again – and make money – and lose it. And round and round they go, unable to retain their wealth. When I meet these entrepreneurs, and they begin to talk about themselves and their business, I often find that they are trying to build businesses that are not congruent with their personal values or philosophies.

If a dishonest person has the job of administering a pension fund, the pension fund may, in the short term, make a lot of money. The administrator might accrue funds and build up a very healthy balance. But then his 'philosophy' will get the better of him. He will not be able to withstand the temptation and his hand will soon be deep within the proverbial cookie jar. The pension fund's objective – to secure people's future income – is not compatible with a person whose personal belief is 'wealth at any cost'. For the same reason, a priest is not the best person to run a brothel!

The point is clear. Your personal philosophy and values have to be in alignment with the business you are in. If they are not, it's likely that your business will falter.

Aligning your philosophy and your business

Have you ever steered a small boat? The key to going forward is to make sure that the rudder, the mechanism that controls the direction of the boat, is aligned with the bow, or front, of the boat. If the rudder is not pointed in the same direction, the boat will go round and round in circles. It is the same with a business. The rudder is the values of the business owner; the boat is the values of the business. And, just as with a boat, if the personal values of the person running the business do not align with the values of the business, it will end up going round and round. In an ideal world, the people evaluating business plans would have an opportunity to check for congruence between the values of the entrepreneur and those of the business. Unfortunately, as we know, in the real world, decisions – particularly rejections – are often made without the funders even meeting the entrepreneur. But a business plan can never highlight the harmony between the values of the entrepreneur and the business. It is very hard to see 'heart' and 'passion' (or lack thereof) in the pages of a business plan. Personally, I could never invest in a business without meeting the entrepreneur and uncovering whether there is alignment between him and the business he wishes to launch.

Philterlosophy

'Philterlosophy' is a term I coined to describe the process whereby entrepreneurs use their personal *philosophy*, in combination with their *filters*, to guide almost every business decision they make. Like Kroc and Ackerman, disciplined entrepreneurs use their philterlosophy as the criterion for making their decisions. If an opportunity arises that does not make it through the philterlosophy, then the opportunity is deemed a threat and the entrepreneur is able to reject it, no matter how tempting it may seem.

One of my mentors, a very wealthy private equity player, makes his investment decisions by asking three simple questions: Do I like the entrepreneur? Will the entrepreneur take some risk? Is the business model sound? And that's it – he will not make an investment unless the answer to all three questions is 'yes'. He has sufficient trust in himself, and his filtering questions, not to waste time vacillating and pondering over decisions.

Raizcorp's philterlosophy is also based on three simple questions. Before we make any decision at Raizcorp, we ask ourselves: 'Is it replicable; is it unique; and is it highly profitable?' Through a long and ever-evolving process, each of these filters has become defined and measurable.

Raizcorp's filters are firmly aligned with my personal philosophy. Let's look at each of them:

- ■ **Unique**
  I've never wanted to just 'fit in', to be a part of the crowd. And I've never been average – I've always

found myself in situations where I am extremely above average or extremely below average.

■ **Profitable**
I was brought up to believe that I deserved to be wealthy. I was never taught that 'rich is only for someone else'.

■ **Replicable**
My whole business career has been about growing businesses. In order to grow, one needs the ability to replicate processes and systems.

And so I have found a way to make sure that all the components of Raizcorp's philterlosophy fit in with my personal philosophies and values. At Raizcorp, the way we recruit, how we conduct our business, our purchasing policies, our clients and our physical premises are all unique, replicable and able to generate profit.

In 2007, Raizcorp moved to new offices. The move was truly an exercise in philterlosophy. From designing the new space to the choice of colours, every decision was made by answering the questions, 'Is it replicable; is it unique; and is it highly profitable?' If it was, we did it; and if it wasn't, we didn't or designed a plan to make it congruent with our philterlosophy.

Every business in Raizcorp is encouraged to develop its own philterlosophy: no more than three words that are representative of the entrepreneur's personal philosophy, and which act as filters to facilitate the decision-making process. And these words are embodied in every facet of the business – from micro to macro.

Two rules

Two rules apply to the choice of words for a philterlosophy. The first rule is self-evident – the philterlosophy has to align with your personal philosophy.

The second rule is that each criterion has to be measurable, either comparatively or empirically.

Every aspect of our business is documented and photographed. In this way, we make sure that Raizcorp is completely replicable. At Raizcorp, we regard a 40% return on investment as highly profitable. If a venture cannot bring us that 40%, or save us 40%, we will pass it over. And, on every level, we are unique when measured against other incubators in South Africa. When Raizcorp first started, 'unique' was measured against other South African incubators. We now measure ourselves against international incubators.

In fact, our philterlosophy changed Raizcorp to such an extent that we had to find a new way to describe what we do. And so we coined the term 'prosperator'. We don't incubate; we prosperate. The word 'incubator' tends to imply sickness and weakness and I don't want to see the companies we work with in this way. Also, 'incubate' suggests a temporary situation. Raizcorp enters into lasting relationships with our partner companies in order to make them profitable.

So, as your business grows and succeeds, so too do your filters help you and your business to evolve and change.

Using your filters to make decisions easily

When you are starting out as an entrepreneur, it might be easy to make decisions. As your business grows and becomes successful, the volume and complexity of the decisions will increase – taking up more and more of your time. Many entrepreneurs become paralysed by the number of decisions they have to make. Taking action becomes difficult. But when you operate through your philterlosophy, you begin to make decisions more easily, allowing you to act with confidence and speed.

Developing a philterlosophy takes time and effort. Some companies in Raizcorp take years to develop their philterlosophy. That time is well spent and is a worthwhile investment because, once they have developed their philterlosophy, their business takes a leap forward. Once you 'get' your philterlosophy, it starts to work for you and your business. When you and your employees operate through your philterlosophy, you will find yourselves taking action and making good business decisions easily.

PART 3

Getting started

Finding your passion

As entrepreneurs, we are passionate about our particular concept or idea. We find an angle or a gap, and then pursue it. As we begin to share our idea with others, we become bewildered when they don't share or, sometimes, don't even understand our idea. 'They just don't get me' is a refrain you will hear often from entrepreneurs.

All too often, we become incredibly frustrated and decide that the whole world is against us. Entrepreneurs need to understand a simple truism: Most people don't 'get' most people.

'I had sex last night'

In my workshop, I divide the group into pairs and allow three minutes for each person to write down words *they* associate with the word 'sex'. Sex is, after all, a universal activity, undertaken by people across all cultures, religions and races. Each person then compares answers with their partner in the group. One would expect that members of a particular group would view sex in essentially similar ways, and so would have a similar interpretation of what sex is all about. The results of the exercise are illuminating.

Up to 10% of the paired-up people have absolutely no words in common. There are instances where each partner writes down up to 20 words without a single correlation. In my experience, the average correlation is less than 14%.

The point is simple – we can't even assume a common understanding in a straightforward statement like 'I had sex last night'. How, then, can you assume that other people will understand your ideas when you try to sell them something as unique as your business concept? Entrepreneurs need to be aware that, even though they themselves can see the value of an idea that they are passionate about, other people generally will not immediately understand or appreciate it. You should not expect the responsibility for understanding the idea to lie with others; the onus is on you to ensure that you are expressing yourself clearly so that you are able to excite others about your business concept. This is why, when entrepreneurs need to produce a business plan, the last place they should go is to a third party. Entrepreneurs must understand, and be able to articulate, their business themselves. A business plan, written by an intermediary, will never have the entrepreneur's 'DNA' within it. And if the investor does not 'get' the idea, the fault lies not with the investor; it lies with the entrepreneur who is relying on someone else to convey his business concept. I sit on many investment boards and I always insist on meeting the entrepreneur before making an investment decision. Too often the conclusions I reach from reading the business plan are completely the opposite of those I reach when I actually meet the entrepreneur.

Focus and passion

When they start out, most entrepreneurs tend to be very unfocused. They don't understand exactly what it is that they do – what added value are they offering? When small businesses start, they tend to try to be 'all things to all people'. They very seldom have focus because their thinking (and it is bad thinking) is 'I can't afford not to do what the client might want me to do'. Inevitably, with this kind of attitude, many of the opportunities that come along are jobs that you are not passionate about, jobs that you are not good at. The clients will take advantage of this to get incredibly cheap rates from you. This not only distracts you from your focus but you spend time and effort doing jobs you don't enjoy for little reward. All that time and effort would be better put towards something that is within your passion, and is within your focus and that you are good at.

I once came across a business called Sandy's Gear Lock and Jewellery. To me, that was the epitome of the small entrepreneur who was trying to be 'all things to all people'. People could go to Sandy's Gear Lock and Jewellery to have a gear lock fitted to their vehicle and, if they needed to buy some jewellery, they could get that there too. It wasn't very long before Sandy's Gear Lock and Jewellery closed down, for obvious reasons. As the saying goes, Jack-of-all-trades and master of none – entrepreneurs who try to offer too wide a range of products or services usually end up doing work that they are not passionate about or are not very good at. Once you get into the mindset of earning an income by providing clients with a product or service that you are not good at, it becomes very hard to escape because you begin to view this income as vital to your existence. And, while this income may indeed be vital to your business, it is also the reason that you will not be able to move forward. Although you would like to have other business more in line with your focus, you will be so busy doing the business that you are not good at that you won't have time to look elsewhere. You may even develop certain competencies in other areas so that you become completely sidetracked and never ever follow your true passion.

Many entrepreneurs, when you ask them what they do, will give you a list of about 15 different things. Take the example of an advertising agency whose owner will tell you, 'We do design; we do print; we do advertising; we do voice-over, we can do whatever you need'. The reality is that the agency outsources most of these things and they do not really do them at all. But entrepreneurs think that the more they offer, the more widely spread their net will be and the more likely they are to catch a big fish. I encourage people not to do this.

When a struggling entrepreneur seeks my advice, I try to understand, first of all, what he and his employees actually do themselves, in-house, and therefore what skills are available within the business. Anything that is outsourced does not form part of the core competency of the business.

The second thing I would push for is for the entrepreneur to start focusing on an area of core competency where their passion lies. If Sandy were to come to me for advice, the first thing I would do is make him choose between jewellery and gear locks!

Focus: A word of caution

It is not always possible, particularly in the early stages of a business, to be as focused as you would like to be. I am a realist and I know, from my own experience, that there are times when cash is so short that any business is good business. At one point, in Raizcorp's early years, we were so desperate for cash that I decided to do public speaking for money. At one of my speaking engagements, I met Leon who was also speaking at the event in order to supplement an income from his also-struggling small business. A few years later, it is only on the odd occasion that I take on speaking engagements and I usually use them to advertise Raizcorp; the motive is no longer cash. Leon has closed his business and is now solely a professional public speaker, but is, sadly, still battling.

Unlike Leon, I invoiced for my talks in Raizcorp's name. Despite the temptation to pocket the money myself, every cent I made went to building my business. I continued only to draw my salary. Leon did not see his speaking in this way. In his mind, the money that he made from public speaking was his; he did not use it to sustain and grow his business. There are times, on the path to building your business, when you may need to look elsewhere for income. A temporary loss of focus is alright but be careful that it does not divert you from your original path. Quick and easy money is a great temptation. If you see the money as a means to an end, you will not lose focus; if money becomes the end in itself, you may soon find yourself in a completely different business!

What is your true passion?

Most people don't really understand what they are truly passionate about. Those who do know their passion often have a strange aversion to making money from it. For some reason they believe that their passion, whether it is for a sport or gardening or even a pet, is merely a hobby, and that business ideas should come from some other place.

A stamp collector may be passionate about stamps; he may be passionate about the process of collecting; or he may be passionate about stamp collecting. If he also collects spoons and cups and books, then he is most probably not so much passionate about stamp collecting as he is about the actual process of collecting things. Most people don't push themselves far enough to discover exactly what it is they are passionate about.

Many self-help books and business gurus will tell you that you have to have passion; they confidently proclaim the merits and virtues of passion. So we look at what we do and we reverse-engineer our lives in order to convince ourselves that we truly are passionate about what we do. A young entrepreneur who runs a small payroll services company recently tried to tell me that he's passionate about payslips. But when I saw him at a party spinning records for his friends, I suspected that his passion may lie elsewhere. Yet another entrepreneur informed me that he was passionate about IT. To which I responded, 'What exactly are you passionate about? The boxes? The wires? The code?' He understood my point.

We rarely take the time to fully understand the essence of what we are passionate about. I know a man who listed his waste disposal company on the Stock Exchange. I cannot imagine that he had a passion for garbage, or grew up looking at the dustbin in his mother's kitchen and saying, 'One day all this garbage will be mine. I love garbage'. However, even as a young child, he kept his room immaculate. He simply enjoyed tidying, cleaning and creating order. And, strange as it sounds, the waste disposal business became a means of expressing his passion. He found a way of making money out of tidying up. Weird? Perhaps, but I've heard of far weirder passions, and met people who have been very successful in identifying, and following, their passion.

Finding your inspiration

Many people want to become entrepreneurs but claim that nothing truly inspires them. They say that there's nothing they *really* understand, that there's no business they have in mind. 'I just want to get into (a) business,' they say.

Inspiration can come from anywhere. The key is to keep an open mind. Many entrepreneurs, when asked where they got their inspiration, have a story to tell of how they found their inspiration in the most obscure of places.

I used to jog along the Durban beachfront. I was 25 years old and I had been offered the opportunity of a lifetime – funding for any business idea that I could develop a sound business model for (I had already passed my mentor's other filter – he liked me!). While jogging, my thoughts would turn to what business I wanted to get into. What was I passionate about? One morning as I jogged, I noticed discarded fast-food packaging along the pathway. Perhaps a fast-food franchise, I thought to myself. Jogging puts me in a trance-like state, and I erroneously convinced myself that I was passionate about fast food. I like it, I buy it, I eat it, was my rationalisation. I started thinking about what I could possibly do differently in the fast-food industry. I eventually came up with a business idea to start the first hot dog chain in South Africa. Was I passionate about fast food? Not really. But I was really passionate about growing a business; I was passionate about doing something new and unique. Even though my inspiration came from something as humble as a fast-food wrapper, it was the spark that culminated, twelve months later, in a business called *The New York Sausage Factory*.

We need to open our minds to the fact that inspiration probably won't come from only one source. I have not yet come across an individual who can claim never to have been inspired by a book, a person, or a movie. We need to understand the basis of that inspiration. What is it about that book, or that person, or that movie that inspired you? When you understand that, you begin to understand what it is that turns you on.

Once you understand what you're passionate about, and your mind is open, inspiration can come from *anywhere*. You are *then* ready to begin the process of actually finding the business idea.

Finding the gap

In my training workshop, I ask participants to look through a newspaper and use its contents to inspire an idea that they believe can be turned into a business opportunity. A group of 30 to 40 people will find 30 to 40 different business ideas out of the same newspaper. When you analyse the ideas, you begin to understand that people find business opportunities based on the way that they view the world at that time. Someone with a leaking tap will notice the article on plumbing problems. He will put forward a plumbing or home maintenance business. The avid gardener will pick out the article about spring coming soon and will present a nursery as a business idea.

At first, when I ask the participants why they have come to that particular business idea, they are not sure. But if I probe hard enough, I usually find that the source of the idea can invariably be traced back to an opportunity or a situation in their own life experience. There is almost always a self-referencing element to the ideas or opportunities that we identify for businesses.

I call this power of self-reference the Red BMW Syndrome. If you buy a red BMW, you almost instantly become aware of hundreds of other red BMWs on the road, which you never noticed before. In the same way, when you are highly aware of what inspires you, you are more likely to find opportunities around you that satisfy that inspiration.

Most people do not push their ideas to the limit to find the gap. They settle for what they believe is good enough.

I once mentored Gerald, a young man who ran a matric dance after-party business. There is a tremendous market for this service. I was amazed to discover that matric dances begin as early as March and continue almost to November. Every weekend Gerald would hold an after-party. I asked him to tell me about his business – he said he organised 'matric dance after-parties'. I asked whether he had any competition in this market – he said he did. I asked what made the schools choose his after-party service rather than the opposition's – and it came down to factors such as his personality, the entertainment he offered, and the quality of his DJs. Invariably, whatever Gerald was offering was copied by the competition, so there was no real protectable gap. It became apparent that this was not really a business capable of expanding in the future because, as time went by, more and more people would enter the market, making it more difficult for Gerald to make money.

We worked solidly trying to find a Unique Selling Proposition (USP) for his business. He kept telling me that his business simply organised matric dance after-parties. I pushed him and pushed him. I made him walk around the building; we looked through magazines to find other angles that might bring inspiration for what could make his business different. The more I pushed, the more he fought back; he insisted that he could find no way to differentiate his business from others.

I continued to challenge him and, at the point where he nearly cracked, he said, in exasperation, 'All I do is market to the youth!' And, finally, the penny dropped. 'So you're a youth marketer,' I replied. 'That's very different from being a thrower of matric dance after-parties.'

I showed Gerald that, once he reclassified himself as a youth marketer, he could approach specific companies in order to market their products and services to young people. Inspiration struck! One of the newest entrants into the cellphone market was specifically targeting the youth market. We approached the cellphone company with a proposal and raised a very large sum in sponsorship for his matric dance after-parties. Suddenly, his business had the ability to offer a far superior party experience, with the best venues and the best events, thereby obliterating the opposition. The company developed an amazing website, provided professional invitations and offered the best DJs (who should have signed agreements exclusively with Gerald). Needless to say, the company's market share grew substantially.

Simply by changing his view of his market, by changing his understanding that he was not simply in the business of organising matric dance after-parties but rather a youth marketing company, the prospects of growing the business were that much greater. Suddenly, he was throwing parties for 45 000 kids a year. This was very exciting to corporate businesses interested in selling their products or services to the youth market.

When you push the idea by not just settling for what you think you do, and you look at it from a different angle, you begin to find new and exciting ways to make money. Not surprisingly, ten years later, Gerald runs a successful logistics business. He has found a way to turn his passion for being organised, and for organising others, into profit. When you're clear about your passion and inspiration, you begin to tune into the world differently – you begin to tune into opportunity.

PART **4**

Tune into
opportunity

Listen for the opportunity

Most business schools teach people to do business in a certain way. Traditional teaching tells us that the individual or team comes up with an idea for a product or a service. It even shows us how to come up with ideas using skills such as brainstorming and lateral thinking. We learn how to get the product produced and how to get the financial backing to build the factory to manufacture the product. Finally, we are taught how to take the product to the market, and how to sell it.

However, in my experience, the majority of successful entrepreneurs do not make their money in the way that schools or universities teach. In fact, I think the way they build their businesses is the complete opposite of this rationale. Entrepreneurs exist within a network – and it is this network that is their potential market (or their route to the market). Entrepreneurs are more likely to see or hear about an opportunity within their own market space. This opportunity may become apparent when talking to friends and colleagues. Someone might mention that he is having problems with a particular aspect of his business, or that he is looking for a particular skill or solution to a problem he is facing. Invariably, the entrepreneur will be in the market at the time that the opportunity arises. He will see the opportunity there and then. The entrepreneur does not come up with an idea, but rather he identifies an *opportunity*. The market is therefore relatively guaranteed because his association with the person who mentioned the opportunity provides the 'in'. The entrepreneur already understands that there is a need for the product or service. He does not have to create the market as it potentially exists already. All that is then required is to produce the solution for the market. He can achieve this in one of two ways. He can build the company required to produce the goods or he can outsource the manufacture of the product for sale into the market.

Keith is a friend of mine who cooks the most delicious food I have ever tasted. He really has a natural relationship with food – he just knows how to combine fresh ingredients to create flavour and taste. Food is his inspiration and cooking is his passion. And the more people he cooked for, the more he heard people saying how much they hated cooking and how they struggled to cook for themselves or their families every day. So Keith began preparing meals, freezing them in suitable portions and selling them to his friends and colleagues. It is a great business concept and, slowly, Keith is increasing his clients and market. But he started with the people he knew – he did not create meals and then take them to market. The demand was there and Keith saw an opportunity.

Keith established demand before he created the supply. I call this demand-side entrepreneurship because the demand already exists. Traditionally, we are taught to produce the supply and then create the demand. This subtle difference is very significant in terms of the way we approach things. It is a mindset.

Entrepreneurs should ideally be looking for opportunities rather than ideas.

Create the opportunity

I began this section by talking about the need for entrepreneurs to 'find' the opportunity. Of course, not everyone is able to do this. Some entrepreneurs need to 'create' the opportunity. For these entrepreneurs, the key lies in research. Research is a critical component of finding the opportunity. These days conducting research is simple – the Internet is the obvious first port of call, followed closely by the plethora of magazines, newspapers, books and trade publications available in the Information Age in which we are privileged to be living. However, merely surfing the web or reading books is not enough. There are a number of ways to conduct research that can significantly improve the process.

The dos and don'ts of research

Do research with a childlike mindset

We have all been in the company of a child who has just discovered the word 'why' – the child who takes nothing at face value. For this child, the world is full of unexplained phenomena, and adults (seemingly) have the answers to all the questions. Very few adults have the discipline to ask why something is being done the way it is. Why do we have to do it that way? The real pioneers are the ones who do not accept that things have to be done a certain way and are prepared to break rules that have been set up. You need to research with a childlike mindset and keep asking questions. What are the established assumptions based on? People generally do things in a certain way because that's how it has been done before, and not because that's the right way to do it now. The fact that we have known – for over 500 years – that the sun doesn't actually rise and set on us, has not changed our worldview. We now know that the earth spins around the sun, yet we still 'see' sunrise and sunset. We write poetry about it; we even sing about it! It was not until Copernicus asked 'why' that humanity gained a better understanding of its place in the universe and where the earth is in relation to the other celestial bodies. But old habits die hard! When you conduct your research, be a child, continually ask why the author of the research says what he does and then ask yourself: 'Is it really true?' When you look at the research with a cynical mindset and begin to deconstruct some of the assumptions, you are more likely to find fresh and different 'angles' and ideas. Research based on false 'facts' promulgates new false facts. In the uncovering of these false facts, lies huge opportunity.

Don't believe the infallibility of the assumptions

While research is a very important component of entrepreneurial life, there are dangers in doing too much research. Once you start researching, you will find that there are bodies of information that repeat conventional wisdom in different variations or interpretations. Once you read something three or four times in different formats, you may very well start to believe the assumptions to be infallible. When something is repeated again and again, it becomes very difficult to challenge the authenticity, or the truth, of those assumptions. It's not impossible, but it becomes more difficult. Too much research will make it tougher for you to find weaknesses in the assumptions.

Don't engage in a never-ending search

Another danger of too much research is that you will not stop. I have a friend who engages in ongoing research, and never quite engages in life. He never quite starts whatever he needs to start because he believes he hasn't gathered enough information.

83

He simply carries on researching and, the more information he gets, the more he realises that he needs more information, and so it becomes an endless loop of non-achievement.

My belief is that many people who want to start a business simply don't have the courage to take the first step. They hide behind their research as a way to explain to their friends and family why they haven't started their business. They always need more time to find a little more information. They hide behind the veneer of being thorough, of being 'perfectionists' (as discussed earlier), when the real truth is they are just too afraid to actually start. I am very cynical when I meet people who have been researching something for five years, or ten years sometimes, and haven't actually started. They don't have the courage to take the risks which the entrepreneurial choice demands.

Don't become intimidated by the results of your research

A great example of being intimidated by the results of research is the fourteenth-century sailor looking to sail across the ocean. Upon doing research, the sailor found that there were apparently dragons at certain places. The Old Dutch mapmakers used to write 'Here Be Dragons' at places where no one had yet visited. The sailor, undertaking research, who saw 'Here Be Dragons' and believed it, would be intimidated by that research, and wouldn't venture there.

If Columbus had been intimidated by the fact that people said the earth was flat, or there were dragons, he wouldn't have reached America.

Don't fall in love with your ideas and then get married to them

All too often, entrepreneurs say 'EUREKA! I've found my idea!' and are so adamant that this is the idea that is going to take them forward, that they aren't prepared to realistically analyse whether or not the idea is commercially viable.

Years ago, a colleague of mine lost his young child on a busy beachfront. After a frantic search that, thankfully, led to his finding the child, he came up with an idea. What if there was a device that parents could use to help them find a lost child? It could be attached to a child's arm and connected to a control box so that at the push of a button the device would light up and sound an alarm making it easy to see where the child was. The fear and worry he experienced while looking for his child provided him with the inspiration to follow up on his idea. After searching on the Internet, he found that such a device already existed and that, instead of re-inventing the wheel, he could import the product. He sent e-mails to the manufacturers in an attempt to secure rights for the product. However, at the same time, one of the largest cellphone companies in the country had developed a similar product, and started to launch it nationally. He realised that he could not compete with this and bowed out of the venture.

Quite coincidentally, at exactly the same time, another entrepreneur approached me with the same idea. I pointed out that the cellphone company had already entered the market and had introduced a similar product. He responded by saying that the phone company's product had only been in the market for a couple of months, was probably his only competition, and that his system was more useable and safer. He had completely convinced himself that he was going to produce a superior product. With no means, no resources, no unique selling proposition, he wanted to compete with the country's largest cellphone company and beat them at their own game. No amount of persuasion on my part could budge him. He was adamant that this was a good idea.

This is a classic example of someone who has fallen in love with his idea. He's thought about it; he's told his friends; he's told his family. They have all said, 'What a fantastic idea!', which has inspired him even more, and when he comes across information that totally annihilates the business case, he will not shift; he will not move; he wants to pursue it nonetheless.

Many entrepreneurs have the same outlook. They simply don't want to look at the facts.

Don't neglect your opposition

The final research tip that I would like to give you is to use your opposition as a source of research. You need to study your opposition. Observe them to see how they are running their businesses with a view to understanding both their weaknesses and their strengths. Then try to put together strategies for your own business that will overcome their weaknesses, and improve on their strengths!

Talk to your competitor's customers. Find out what their view is. Chat to people about your idea and ask them what they think of it. Do they think it would work? Why or why not?

Become a customer of the opposition and experience the process of buying a product or service from them. If you have several different competitors, try to be a customer of as many of those competitors as you possibly can, and see where their strengths and weaknesses lie.

Ray Kroc, founder of the McDonald's Corporation, spent enough time in restaurant kitchens to know that, behind the scenes, food got dropped on the floor and then picked up and served! By creating completely visible food preparation areas, he ensured that his customers knew that at McDonald's cleanliness was a priority. 'If you've got time to lean, you've got time to clean' became their mantra. McDonald's exploited a weakness that was very common in the industry – that the customer could not see what went on in the kitchen. Simply showing customers how organised their kitchens were gave them a competitive advantage. Observing his opposition gave him one of the ideas that turned McDonald's into the brand it is today. McDonald's now has coffee bars in its franchises. They continue to remain one step ahead of their opposition all the time, keeping their eyes firmly on their competition, even when the competition is as unapparent as a chain of coffee shops!

Pose different questions

So you've found your passion, you've done your research, and you think you're onto something good. Now, you need to start considering what it is that makes your product or service unique. The way to do this is to look at your offering from different angles.

When I work with entrepreneurs, I challenge them to ask what I call 'different' questions. I would like to challenge you, before you read on, to do the same thing about your business product, service or idea. The exercise is about looking at things differently in order to find the angle that makes your business unique. The questions are intended to stimulate your mind so that you come up with ideas that you would not necessarily think about in the normal course of setting up, or improving, your business.

These are the questions I pose:

1. Imagine your product or service as a software package. What features would the product have, and what would be the benefits of these features?

2. How would your business be different if you were a paraplegic in a wheelchair?

3. How would your business be different if you were based in the Bahamas?

4. How would your business be different if your working hours were from 6pm to 6am?

5. What would be different about your business if you served a home-cooked meal at every single meeting?

Now that you're (hopefully) satisfied that you've considered your business from the different angles outlined above, let's look at the ideas behind each of the questions and how they can help you in growing your business.

1. We often see software packages packed in boxes and displayed for sale. If your business could be packaged and sold in this way, what would your box look like? What words would be on the box? Would there be a flash that says 'now with XYZ', or 'new and improved'? This is a tough question. Most people can't imagine their businesses as a box on a shelf. However, this is a really useful question to answer if you want to understand your unique selling proposition – because that's exactly how the end-users will be looking at your business when deciding whether to buy into it or not. The people who are going to be using your product or service look at how well it is packaged. Is the software package used for word processing? Is it spreadsheet software? Is it anti-virus? You need to package your product so that the buyer understands exactly what it is. The software package will be put on a shelf, among other similar competitive packages. In order for consumers to establish the best product to buy, they need to be able to see clearly what the product's unique features and benefits are. As an entrepreneur, you need to go through the process of deciding what

your product or service will look like. You cannot expect someone to buy into your idea until you know what it is you are selling.

2. When I ask entrepreneurs to consider their business from the point of view of a paraplegic, what they find, besides obvious answers such as having access ramps, is that they would have to be far more efficient in the way they operate; and, because they are wheelchair-bound, they would want to travel less. In addition, a person in a wheelchair would have to be more efficient in their communication with clients and staff. Another interesting point that emerges from this exercise is that over 40% of the respondents believe that being a paraplegic would allow them to do a lot more than they are currently doing. This is a very surprising outcome. I think that it is because being disabled would, ironically, empower them in a way that being able-bodied does not. There is a certain courage, a perspective that comes with being a paraplegic, that gives strength. The obvious question then is: 'Why can't you do those things now while you're able-bodied?' Participants usually get a puzzled look on their faces. They realise that they had simply never thought of their business that way before.

3. The idea behind the Bahamas question is simple. The Bahamas is a group of remote islands with a small population and economy. If somebody wanted to run a business from the Bahamas, they would require Internet connectivity, and would need to market their business using the

Internet. There would be a need to travel in order to find new markets for their products or services. Furthermore, working on an island may mean a lower propensity for hard work and a higher inclination for relaxing. In such circumstances, finding the motivation to drive the business would become crucial. Alternatively, being in a place you love may give you just the motivation you need to drive your business! How would that affect the course of your venture?

4. The question about working from 6pm to 6am poses a completely new set of issues. For example, since most people work normal business hours, and you would be working at night, you could not communicate with people during the day. How then do you leave messages? How do you meet people? What process do you use to meet people, or sell your products, or find markets for your product, when you don't work in the same time zone as your traditional market? This prompts many people to think of looking at international markets for their product. People start realising that they are not limited to their local market for their product or service; the fact that they work from 6pm to 6am actually becomes an advantage as international markets are far bigger than local markets.

5. Lastly, regarding serving a meal at every meeting, the obvious answer here is that you'd get fat! Once they get beyond this answer, I find that people believe that they would have better communication with their clients, as food is a catalyst for

communication in most cultures. Families, for example, get together at meal times. Suddenly, the concept of serving food at every meeting equates to better communication! When your clients feel special, satisfied and nurtured, you might just find it easier to make the sale. Ask yourself: What else could I do to make my clients feel this way?

I find that, in the process of working through these questions, people's minds start opening to a different type of reality. Instead of thinking linearly in respect of their current lives and opportunities, new possibilities unfold simply by asking questions that force them to look at their business from different angles. By answering these questions, entrepreneurs learn that by asking different questions they begin to open themselves up to new and different possibilities. When you ask the right type of questions, you can dramatically alter current realities.

PART **5**

Raising money

'Where's the washing?'

Most entrepreneurs begin with the premise that their start-up business needs money. But, in most instances, what the business actually needs is a paying customer and a compelling economic reason to exist. Thembi recently approached a member of my team with the notion that she wanted to open a laundry. She needed the mentor's help to secure funding to open her laundry. Thembi had done her research, found a location and believed that she needed a substantial amount of money to buy all the equipment. My colleague questioned her on her research and Thembi was adamant. She had spoken to many people and they had all promised her that they would indeed bring their laundry to her. My colleague, while not detracting from her excitement, gently suggested that perhaps she was being a bit hasty and suggested a slightly more phased approach. After much discussion, the entrepreneur eventually accepted that perhaps she should begin with one washing machine and a tumble dryer. Her mentor then asked her a very simple question: 'Where's the washing?' He suggested that, before she buys any of her equipment, she needed to secure one bag of washing which she could hand wash and then iron in return for payment. My colleague is still waiting for Thembi to bring him just one bag of paid-for washing!

Teddy Roosevelt's adage, 'If you build it, they will come' is generally not true in the twenty-first century. Too many entrepreneurs have learned the hard way that building it is simply not enough to get the customers in and persuade them to part with their money. You need to have the confidence, as well as some kind of evidence that, once it is built, they will indeed come. That is why I love the question, 'Where's the washing?' It represents the all-important question that all entrepreneurs must ask themselves: 'Where is the demand?' When you have the notion that what you need is money, you forget about the fact that, even with the money, if you do not have a paying customer, the business is not going to succeed. The best form of funding is the free cash flow generated by the profits derived from selling your product or service to customers. I firmly believe that there is more money chasing good, compelling business ideas than there are good, compelling business ideas chasing money. It's better to raise money when you already have a powerful semi-proven business case that requires funding to expand and grow.

I am, however, a realist and I know that there are situations where funding is an upfront requirement to get started. You may need to prepare a business plan. Make sure that the plan is your own and that you have thought through every aspect of your business. In this section, we will explore some of the things you need to know when sourcing finance for your venture.

Make sure you have done your homework

Before you approach investors claiming that your idea is unique, make sure that it really is or you'll be blown out of the water in the first minute. I've seen this happen many times. People approach investors with what they say is a fantastic, never-before-seen idea. Investors, especially venture capitalists, see a tremendous number of business ideas in an average month. Over several years in the industry, they will have seen many more ideas than you can possibly imagine. Claiming to have a unique idea when investors know that it already exists elsewhere communicates to them that you haven't done enough research, and that the investors haven't necessarily come across any would-be competitors. It's important to note that there are very few products or services that do not have any competition. They might not be viewed as classic competition, but they might be considered secondary competition. Secondary competition is a completely different market that might be competing with you for the same share of the customer's budget. So be very careful not to say that your product or service has absolutely no competition.

Keep the slides to a minimum

Too many slides get boring; too few, don't give enough depth. Generally, investors are busy people and they have a short attention span so you need to get to the bottom line very quickly. If you find yourself in a situation where you are asked to do a formal presentation and you want to use PowerPoint to do so, remember eight slides are ideal, 16 slides are too many. You need just enough slides to give a bit of meat and oomph, but not too many to make it tedious. This is another thing that I have learned the hard way.

Investors do not need to know the whole story behind your idea. Fascinating as it may be to you that inspiration struck while you were sitting in the bath, and there was a rubber duck in the bath, and the duck was looking at you, and so on, investors do not want to hear this. By the time you get to the actual point, the investor has lost interest.

As entrepreneurs, we want to tell a great story about our product, we want to share our passion about it, we don't want it boiled down to one little concept. We want to give it depth, and so we tend to tell a long and involved story around the subject matter before we get to the bottom line. Investors, on the other hand, want to get to the bottom line as quickly as possible. My suggestion is that you let them explore your idea and ask the questions. Let the investors discover the opportunity for themselves. Give them the basic facts and let them choose which parts of the presentation they want to discuss. Be very sure that you understand the detail behind the points that you make in your presentation.

Prepare your elevator pitch

How often have you been asked, 'What do you do?' When asked this question, you need to be prepared to give your 'elevator pitch'. Imagine finding yourself in the elevator (lift) with an important person who may very well be in a position to change your life. This person asks you what you do. You then have a very short time, from the time the elevator doors close to the time they re-open, to say your piece and grab his attention. Generally speaking, your elevator pitch needs to be less than 55 seconds – the shorter the better.

It's very important that you work out the essence of what you do, and keep practising it until you have perfected it. In this way, you encourage people to start exploring the concept themselves. You empower people, especially investors, when you let them believe that they are in control of the questions.

Sell yourself more than your plan!

In most of the interactions I've had with investors, I've found that they are generally not interested in the business plan upfront. The plan is almost secondary, if not tertiary. They are looking for the passion; they are looking for your idea. Of course, they are looking to see if the idea is commercially compelling, but first they are looking to see if *you*, the entrepreneur, have the passion and ability to pull it off. Initially, they will be exploring you, the person, more than the business plan. Once they are satisfied that you are the potential champion for the idea, and that the potential custodian of their investment is the right person, then they will go to the second phase, which is to look at the business plan and see if it is viable. They will also generally have other people, such as accountants, who will look at these business plans. So when you arrive at a meeting to sell your idea, do not present your business plan immediately. Certainly you should have it ready and available but it's more important to be prepared and able to explain your business, or business idea, clearly and succinctly and, most importantly, with confidence. You also need to make sure that you are able to demonstrate your ability to adapt if the assumptions change – as they surely will!

Don't include market-related salaries in your business plan

Investors are more comfortable investing if they see that you are also taking a risk. This is a critical point. One of the key determining factors that investors will look at is how much risk you are taking. They are putting up their money and their name behind your business. When you include in your business plan a salary for yourself that is market related, it is a clear indication to them that you are not prepared to make any sacrifice. In most instances, they will be quite prepared to ensure that your salary increases as the profitability of the business increases. But they will not be keen to see you taking a relatively large salary while they are taking all the risk. Ideally, if you can, allocate yourself a zero salary in the business plan, and only introduce payment for yourself in the month that you plan to begin making a profit.

Investors are conservative

Most good investors have enough investment experience to understand that business plans are merely an indication of how the business might develop, given certain parameters. So, they take a far more conservative approach to the numbers. I've met with investors who have a simple policy on this. They look at the business model and then cut the sales by 25–50%, increase the cost-of-sales by 25–50%, and then increase the expenses by 25%. Then, if the model still works, they are prepared to look at the business. They call this adding 'a beta coefficient' – in other words, a degree of risk – to the business model, to see if the business would be sustainable under the most conservative of circumstances.

Investors like barriers to entry

The higher the barriers to entry, the greater the probability of investment. A barrier to entry is an obstacle that makes it difficult for a competing company to enter a market. Investors see barriers to entry as an indicator of higher potential profits and business longevity. Among other things, barriers to entry may take the form of patents, brand dominance and exclusivity contracts. It is important to highlight these barriers to entry to potential investors, with the accompanying evidence.

Investors prefer businesses that can be easily scaled (grown)

A question that investors often ask is, 'Where do you see this business in the next five to ten years?' Investors are looking for high returns. They understand that this is a function of scale, i.e. the ability to grow your business exponentially. They will therefore want to know how you intend to scale your business, in terms of numbers, infrastructure and resources. Before you meet with your potential investor, think through how you will scale your business. Create a scenario in your mind where you have unlimited funding – what would your barriers to growth be and how would you overcome them?

Remember also that scaling business involves a higher degree of complexity in the business model. It is important that you *think through* what these complexities might be.

Know your funder's 'flavour'

Generally, you will find that investors have certain 'flavours' or preferred investments. Some might have a preference for investing in IT companies; some for resources; others for manufacturing. Generally, funders and investors fall into certain categories. So make sure you are not bringing an IT business idea to an investor who has a reputation for only investing in manufacturing. Do your homework before you go to see investors.

Understand your investor's expectations

It is imperative that you understand your investor's expectations with regard to return on investment and exit strategies. Once again, you need to do research: Find out what exactly the investors expect. Are they long-term players? Are they short-term players? Don't be afraid to ask investors what they expect in terms of return on investment. It's not rude to ask this question in your first meeting. In fact, you will probably impress them by showing them that you are thinking along these lines. Some investors do not have exit strategies, and you need to know this. Do they sell back to you? Do they sell to institutions? What is their general modus operandi? Make sure you understand this before entering into any relationship with an investor.

Know the true cost of having an investor

You need to be aware that there are possible downsides to having an investor. Let's look at some of the disadvantages to securing finance for a business venture.

The first (obvious) downside is that you lose equity (your share of ownership in the business). Equity is the most expensive way to raise capital for a business. Initially, it strengthens your balance sheet, and reduces your requirement to pay back debt. But, in the long run, you may regret the extent to which you reduced your equity base.

The second downside is the loss of independence. As a 100% shareholder, you have no obligation to discuss your strategies with anyone, and you don't have to report back to anyone. Many entrepreneurs find that having to report to investors, however informal the reporting structures may be, is something alien to their nature. Many entrepreneurs become entrepreneurs because they don't want a boss – and investors can sometimes seem very 'bossy'!

Many investors will only release funds at predetermined times according to a business plan. Having an investor can mean that the business plan is less flexible and cannot easily be adapted to circumstances. Very often, having proposed a business plan to an investor and secured his investment, things begin to change – markets change and world economies change. All too often, entrepreneurs find that they cannot alter the business plan to accommodate these changes. He who holds the gold holds the power. Even if they have only a small percentage in your business, your investors are supplying the business with cash, and you are dependent on them. They may say: 'If you don't listen to me, I'm taking my money away'.

Of course, there is also an upside to having an investor. Investors can bring a whole new network into play; they can provide a valuable new perspective on your business and will, of course, provide investment and growth capital to your business.

I believe that intelligent capital is the best form of investment. In this instance, one receives capital as well as business advice, mentoring and support.

The combination is far more powerful than money alone.

Bootstrapping your business

Sometimes, financing your business with your own limited money is better than sourcing funding. This is called bootstrapping, i.e. running your business on a very low budget. When you bootstrap your business, you reveal the weaknesses in it. There is no room for 'make-believe' in businesses with very little cash flow. All the potential flaws – in profitability, delivery, cash-flow management – become apparent. As soon as cash is injected into a business, these weaknesses become less apparent. Huge inefficiencies can be covered up in a business that is being financed. The injection of cash hides these inefficiencies – but not for long.

While it's important to understand that taking on investors may be the most important thing that you ever do in your business, and that it can lead to untold wealth, it's essential to choose the right investors. Ideally, you need investors who have an attitude of partnership, who believe that they are in the business with you, who see your vision, and who support and back you in achieving that vision.

Myths about cash

Ifirmly believe that the first and most vital requirement of a successful venture is a paying customer with a need that your business is satisfying. It is ironic that the cash-inflow process (invoicing and debt collecting) – which is possibly the most important part of an entrepreneur's survival – is often the most badly conducted part of a business. There are a number of reasons for this. I call these the entrepreneur's 'myths about cash'. Let's look at some of them. If you are running your own business, you need to make sure you destroy these myths as soon as possible!

Myth 1: The 'big guys' hold the power

I've seen many entrepreneurs get very excited when they land a contract with a large corporate. They do the work in record time; they over-promise and they over-deliver; they submit their invoice – and then the waiting game begins. One month-end rolls into the next, but no payment is received. So excited were they to clinch the deal, and so elated were they that a corporate was giving them business, that they neglected to negotiate any kind of payment terms. And once the work is done, the entrepreneur has no bargaining power left. In the entrepreneur's mind it goes something like: 'They are the big guys; I'm the little guy – I should be grateful for the work. I can't bug them for money – they'll pay when they're ready. They have processes and procurement departments and finance committees and ... and ...' – the list goes on. Too afraid to confront the big guys, the entrepreneur sees his cash flow become an overdraft and, by the time the money comes in, it's already spent! Corporates know how to play the power game and they exploit the power differential. Entrepreneurs need to know this and they need to make sure, upfront, that they negotiate payment terms and get them in writing.

Myth 2: They're busy

Entrepreneurs perceive corporates to be 'very busy, much busier than little ole me'. There is a false perception that corporates and their representatives (the people you deal with) are incredibly 'busy'. In my experience, they are no busier than the entrepreneur who is running his 'small' business. In fact, I think that having to manage every aspect of a business makes the entrepreneur far busier than the corporate employee who has the luxury of being able to focus only on his core area of the business. My advice to entrepreneurs is not to buy into the myth of 'busyness'. If you are owed money, bug the busy guy – he has no more or less time than you!

Myth 3: They're good for the money

When dealing with corporates, many entrepreneurs tend to believe that big businesses are always 'good' for the money. This is not necessarily true. Corporates, like any business, face the same challenges as a small business – they face market difficulties, cash flow issues and competition. They just use more sophisticated terms, such as 'budget cutbacks' or 're-structuring', rather than tell the truth and say that they are unable to pay.

The keys to cash: Confidence and clarity

For the entrepreneur, getting paid is a function of two 'Cs': Confidence and Clarity.

Confidence is the entrepreneur's greatest gift to self. If you believe in the value of your product or service and if you believe that you deserve to be paid – despite the myths outlined previously – then you will approach the transaction with the corporate in a confident and decisive manner. Entrepreneurs who keep themselves small stay small. They act small and they let the 'big guys' get away with unacceptable behaviour. The key is to act big – it may be a cliché but entrepreneurs have to 'fake it till they make it'. Take on the role of the confident supplier. Do not let your customers see your fears and do not give in to feelings of inferiority.

Confidence is only one half of the equation; clarity is the other. Many entrepreneurs find that they do not get paid because of a supposed misunderstanding regarding the terms of engagement. Ideally, the best way to avoid this is through a comprehensive contract. However, this is not always practical. It is therefore very important for the entrepreneur to outline the basic terms of the deal. These terms need to include quantities, qualities, delivery times and, most importantly, payment terms. Doing a credit check is also particularly helpful. Most entrepreneurs are too scared to ask a corporate to complete a credit application. But you are completely within your rights to ask for this! They need you as much as you need them. What looks like a David-and-Goliath situation is often a result of David giving his power to Goliath. Don't do it! Stand firm and confident in your ability to deliver and your right to receive payment with the same haste that you will be expected to deliver the product or service!

What about a partner?

It takes two

To say that we all have strengths and weaknesses is trite. It is, after all, our strengths and weaknesses that give us our individuality. Successful people are able to leverage their strengths to their advantage while accepting their weaknesses as qualities on which they need to work and, hopefully, improve. In the same way that, internally, we have strengths and weaknesses so too, on an external level, life presents us with opportunities and threats. Why, you may ask, am I making these self-evident statements? For me, it is essential that as entrepreneurs, we understand how our strengths and weaknesses interplay in an external world filled with both opportunities and threats.

When we are feeling strong, and an opportunity presents itself, we ride the wave. By the same token, we are clearly at our most vulnerable when, in a moment of internal weakness, an external threat appears. These human characteristics make us susceptible to failure. If we are concurrently threatened and weak, we can, quite literally, be wiped out. Many entrepreneurs quit for this very reason. The combination of the external threat and the internal weakness makes them give up. 'I can't take it anymore' and 'this is too much for me' are often-heard refrains among entrepreneurs. In my experience, the majority of entrepreneurs who do not succumb when they are most vulnerable are the ones who are operating in partnership. And the reason is quite simple: Partners are able to act as buffers for each other so that, when one partner is feeling down, the other is able to assume the position of strength. At the same time, when an opportunity arises, the strong partner (at that moment) is able to make sure that it is not missed. Wagner and Muller, in their book *The Power of 2*,[v] cite the examples of Steve Jobs and Steve Wozniak of Apple, Bill Gates and Paul Allen of Microsoft, and Bill Hewlett and David Packard of HP to back up the latest research that start-ups, driven by a partnership, are more likely to succeed. According to the authors, two is the magic number.

In my mind, there is no doubt that a shared entrepreneurial endeavour results in the creation of a bigger business than one run by a 'lone wolf'. Even though, at times, a partnership may take strain, the benefits of a good partnership outweigh the potential pitfalls of taking on a partner.

The evolution of the partnership

Many partnerships evolve naturally as two, or even three, people begin the business together. Usually acquaintances or friends, they begin talking, formulate an idea and then start their business. This is the 'same place; same time' type of partnership.

In other cases, one person has the idea but recognises that he doesn't have the requisite skills, contacts or money, and so he approaches someone with whom to partner. This is the 'I need you; you need me' type of partnership.

In both of the above cases, the partners are present at the origin of the business.

The third type of partnership is when a 'lone wolf' – in a business that already exists – approaches a partner to bolster the weaknesses or perceived gaps in the business. This is not unlike the 'I need you; you need me' type of partnership but, here, the timing of the partnership is different.

Who will lead?

The above types of partnerships illustrate that, generally, entrepreneurial businesses create their leadership structures in very unscientific, disorganised ways. So, for example, in the 'same place; same time' type of partnership, the partner who is perceived to have the most important skills generally becomes the perceived leader. So, in an engineering business, started by an engineer and a marketer, the engineer will probably assume the leadership mantle. In the 'I need you; you need me' type of partnership, generally speaking the one with the most money takes on the leadership role. This is not always true but, in my experience, 'he who has the gold makes the rules'.

Then there is the third and, unfortunately, all-too-common form of leadership in an entrepreneurial partnership. This is the 50-50 egalitarian style of leadership. I call this 'entrepreneurship-as-democracy'. These businesses have co-managing directors, with neither partner willing to grab the reins of leadership. In my experience, no matter how the partnership evolved, this type of partnership is doomed to fail. In any business, there can only be one designated leader. Without this acknowledgement by the partners, the business is literally a ship without a captain.

Decisions need decision-makers

In the start-up phase, entrepreneurial businesses are very fragile. Decision-making is crucial. A business that cannot make decisions, and adapt quickly, will not survive. When partners need to consult each other about every single decision, where partners are too afraid to make decisions and no one wants to hurt anyone's feelings, you either have an argument, a stalemate or both. Small businesses cannot afford to hesitate and delay at every turn but, more importantly, it is essential that they make the right decisions. In the start-up phase, the potential impact of decisions is huge. An established business that takes a wrong turn has a greater chance of survival than a start-up company does. A wrong decision, or even a hesitation in making a decision, can sink a small business. One person has to be authorised to 'call it' and take responsibility. I have seen a business where two partners' indecision regarding whether to hire a sales manager led to the demise of the business. They spent so much time in discussions and debates over the matter that their sales took a backseat and, ultimately, there was no business to fight about!

I believe that the best platform on which to forge a partnership is based on the saying 'opposites attract'. The most powerful partnerships occur when two people with different points of view, who have the ability to debate scenarios and outcomes, are able to

119

come together and arrive at decisions that are well-analysed and thought through. I believe that there is less rigour to the decision-making processes in a business where the partners have the same mindset, tend towards the same conclusions, and rarely have the need to debate issues.

Partnerships are particularly useful in times of negotiations. Entrepreneurial partners get to play 'good cop; bad cop' with a greater probability of securing a better deal. Because partners see opportunities and threats in different ways, they are able to perceive the situation differently and, therefore, respond differently. This makes negotiations and deal-making more robust.

In my current partnership, my partner, a chartered accountant, is the 'finance man'; I am the 'marketing man'. Our skill sets are completely different. Decisions in our business, while made quickly, are not made without discussion, analysis and debate. And, once we have heard each others' points of view, we do not allow a stalemate situation to develop. If it is a financial decision, I allow his view to prevail; if it is a marketing decision, he will concede to me. In all other areas, if we absolutely cannot agree, I am the agreed-upon leader and my decision will be respected.

Values and vision

Although I believe that, in terms of skills and personalities, 'opposites' make better partners, where partners do need commonality is in values and vision.

Without shared values, partnerships are very difficult. Partners with different work ethics, for example, are headed for disaster. Although there will almost always be one person who works harder than the other, if the one is leaving to surf at 3 pm every day while the other is working till midnight, the partnership will not survive the bitterness and rancour that will ensue. On the issue of work ethic, there is often a misconception in partnerships that 'the rainmaker does the business make'. In my business, I bring in almost all the business. But I know with certainty that without my partner's ability to bring the deal to legal and final closure, to check the contracts and negotiate the finer details, I would not be able to be out there closing the deals. The fact that the rainmaker can hand over the deal to the other partner to do what he is good at cannot be underestimated. An entrepreneur who believes that, because he is bringing in the work, he can overlook the partner who is executing the work, is not suited to partnership.

Shared vision is another necessity. While in most partnerships, the designated leader may be the one who sets the vision, it is vitally important that the other partner buys, and believes in, the vision. My partner took a lot of convincing! But we dialogued and we shared and, even though he remained sceptical, he trusted me and never denigrated the vision. It was my job to sell it to him. Eventually, as the business grew, he bought into it completely. Without common vision, there is division and when there is division, there is potential for self-destruction. Two partners who are pulling the business in different ways create politics and factions in both management and staff, and that is the beginning of the end of a small business.

Ability and willingness

Another thing to look for in a partner is whether he has both the ability and willingness to take risks.

Ability is simple: you either have the means or you don't. And the means have to be available for the anticipated duration of the risky start-up period.

If both partners have the means, but one is unwilling to invest as much as the other, i.e. his appetite for risk is low, the partnership, in its current form, will not survive.

The rules of engagement: Making the partnership work

There are a few rules that you need to adhere to in order for a healthy partnership to exist within an entrepreneurial business. The first one, which I illustrated above, is that the non-designated leader accept the other's leadership. However, in order for that to work, the designated leader can never take advantage of his authority. This, coupled with a mature ability not to take things personally, lies at the heart of a successful partnership. My partner and I play only the ball, never the man!

Another golden rule is for partners never to criticise each other publicly. Disagreements and squabbles cannot happen in front of the staff. This is the only way to ensure that you have no politics for power in your company. You want to avoid the situation where staff members take sides and play one partner off against another. The best way to prevent 'fighting in front of the children' is for partners to schedule and hold official and regular meetings. I mentored two partners who, because they sat in the same office, chatted over coffee, and overheard each other's phone calls, believed that they were communicating. I insisted that they sit in separate offices and hold weekly, agenda-driven, management meetings. Too often, entrepreneurs do not see themselves as 'professional', mainly because they are conducting their businesses in an amateurish way. Acting and thinking professionally is one of the keys to growing a business!

Another way in which to keep a partnership professional is not to mix your social and business lives. I attend my partner's children's birthday parties, and every now and again we have dinner together with our wives joining us. But, for the rest of the time, we mix in completely different circles. And so it should be. I have seen too many partnerships ruined by over-familiarity. Spouses argue, children fight, employees take sides and, suddenly, the family affairs are affecting the business. Having different social circles is not only healthy but also allows the partners to bring their different experiences and influences to bear on the business. Having both parties 'feeding' from the same sources is not healthy and reduces the amount of new information coming into the business.

A witness to your business

Many of the entrepreneurs who approach Raizcorp for support are SOHO (Small Office/Home

Office) entrepreneurs. More often than not, these entrepreneurs are lonely and feel the need to be part of a community. There is no question that having a business partner is one of the ways to reduce the loneliness that often accompanies the entrepreneurial journey. There is a beautiful scene in the movie *Shall We Dance?* in which the character, played by Susan Sarandon, utters the memorable words: 'We need a witness to our lives ... in a marriage you're promising to care about everything ... the good things, the bad things, the terrible things, the mundane things ... all of it, all of the time, every day. You're saying "Your life will not go unnoticed because I will notice it. Your life will not go un-witnessed because I will be your witness".' Being an entrepreneur is lonely; it helps to have a witness and, not unlike a marriage, it helps when there is someone else who 'cares about everything'.

PART **6**

Building your business

It's not about making money

Once everything is in place – you've found your passion, you have your market, you may even have secured some funding and, hopefully, you have customers willing to pay, you've identified yourself as a growth entrepreneur and your business is up and running – then it's time to build it.

I have a 'secret' for you: If you're going to succeed as a growth entrepreneur, don't focus on making money. That's quite a statement to make. On the surface, it seems like an absolute contradiction – surely we become entrepreneurs to make money!

I have met so many 'entrepreneurs', slowly approaching 60, who find themselves unable to retire or stop working because the minute they stop working, they won't have an income. For me, these entrepreneurs are the lifestyle entrepreneurs I mentioned earlier in the book. They are making money by the hour and, if they are not 'at work' practising their craft, if they get sick or take a holiday, then they are not earning money. This problem does not belong solely to professionals. The reality is that many lifestyle entrepreneurs face the same dilemma: without the owner, there is no business. The entrepreneur and the business are, for all intents and purposes, one and the same thing. If the entrepreneur is having a bad day, the business is having a bad day; if the business has a bad day, the entrepreneur has a bad day. Without the entrepreneur, there is, generally, no value in the business. As long as a successful business still relies heavily on the entrepreneur's input, it has little value. Because the value proposition and, usually, all the client/supplier relationships are held with the entrepreneur, there is no real value in the business without the entrepreneur.

However, successful growth entrepreneurs are able to grow their businesses precisely because they have taken the value proposition of the owner and translated it into systems that allow the business to exist without the owner's direct participation. Profitable and valuable businesses have most, if not all, of the value proposition integrated into the systems and fabric of the business. Think about a huge organisation, such as Anglo American or IBM. If the head of that business goes on holiday, gets sick or even dies, the business continues to run. The share price might take a slight dip, but the business will not crash. Ironically, the CEO of one of the top insurance companies in the world recently left the company – and their share price went up, not down (obviously, an unpopular CEO)!

'What does this have to do with me?' you may be asking. 'I'm running a small business – how can you compare me with Anglo American?' And that is precisely the mindset that keeps entrepreneurial businesses small and, probably, unprofitable.

Build systems

The owner of a company, someone I had mentored, recently decided to emigrate. The company is very successful. But, after more than ten years in business and, despite the fact that she employs more than ten people, the owner is still the business. She is struggling to sell her business because she and the prospective buyers cannot agree on what the business is worth. With her, the business is worth millions; without her, it is very hard to quantify what the business will be worth. She has resisted building systems and processes in the business – and now she is paying the price.

When you begin running a business, you need to spend a tremendous amount of time on creating systems. Of course, if you're spending time developing systems, you aren't going to be using that time to find new business. This seems to contradict conventional business practice. You're trying to grow your market share and I'm proposing that you take valuable time away from finding customers and put it into building the systems in the business. The secret to building a successful business lies in finding a balance between the two.

In a business, systems are an automated way of doing something that has to be done again and again. Let me give you an example. Mike, an entrepreneur I've worked with, employs quite a few salespeople. At first, whenever he needed to employ a new salesperson,

Mike was responsible for the selection process – a process that took up much of his time. So Mike developed a questionnaire that formed part of the interview process. The questionnaire has 20 questions with a separate document showing how to score the answers. So now Mike is able to give these documents to his Sales Manager allowing her to interview the candidates according to the same criteria, and score according to the scoring criteria that he developed. After the interview, the would-be sales person writes a sales test, which Mike developed as well. Now, all this can happen without him. While the Sales Manager is interviewing the candidates, Mike can be out in the market looking for new clients, growing the market share of his business.

How much time does an entrepreneur whose business is beginning to succeed spend interviewing new employees? And, when he finds the right candidate, what will he base his choice on? Will it be gut feel? Personality? Education? Most entrepreneurs won't be able to tell you. They haven't spent any time building the system of bringing new employees into the business. So only the entrepreneur can hire – and that takes time.

The mere fact that Mike has written down the questions, which he knows can be used over and over again, and that he has taken the time, just once, to explain what he is looking for in the answers, means that the process can be repeated without him. As simple as this might sound, the majority of entrepreneurial businesses that I have come across do not do this. So the first thing that I do when I engage with them is to ensure that they understand this process and that they understand the importance of building the systems of their business. When you begin to develop a culture of system building in your business, you will see, very quickly, that you have developed a body of intellectual property that exists within the business. Should you want to sell the business in the future, the value proposition of the business is not embodied in your head but rather in all the systems that the business has developed. You have thus created value for the potential purchaser.

Time to hire ...

To begin building your business you need to look, first of all, at the roles you play. Name them and analyse them. At some point in Raizcorp's history, I was CEO, trainer, marketer, salesman, coach and mentor. In time, I was able to draw up an ever-evolving role description for each of these functions. When, like most entrepreneurs, I found myself stressed and overworked, I knew the time had come to rid myself of one of these roles. I knew I would need to delegate the task of coaching to somebody else. But I did not have the money to hire a coach. The only way I could find the extra money was to increase sales but I couldn't increase sales because I was spending so much time coaching. A real catch-22 situation! I knew that I would have to attract more clients in order to make the money to hire a coach. I put in place a new offering that I knew would increase revenue and, as soon as we got our first clients, I hired the coach. Now, I could really get out and promote Raizcorp to prospective clients who, of course, needed coaching – making my investment in a coach pay for itself.

Think about the various roles you play in your business. What role could you give up? What role would you be able to delegate in order to free yourself up to concentrate on other profit-producing activities? The first question to ask, therefore, is: 'How will this role add to the value proposition of my business?' Then, assign a monetary cost to that role in the form of a salary – how much will it cost you to hire that person?

The next question to ask is: 'When I've employed that person, will I, with the extra time that I have now created, be able to generate the profits needed to pay their salary?' If the answer is 'yes', your business needs that person in order to grow. And if the answer is 'no', you need to ask yourself a more challenging question: 'What do I need to change in the business?' You need to work out how to generate the money that will give you the ability to pay for the person you need to employ.

Zandile runs an arts-based educational company. The only way she can grow her business is to visit schools – something she loves doing. Unfortunately, as she increased her client base, so her paperwork grew and the more she needed to be in the office to take calls. The more time she spent in the office, the less she was able to go out to grow her business. It seemed like a vicious circle because Zandile kept telling herself that she couldn't afford an administrator. But Zandile was basing this assumption on her current rate of growth. With an administrator in the office, Zandile's ability to go out and sell her product would quadruple – allowing her to pay for the administrator and grow her business! Zandile had documented all her business processes and systems and so, when she took the leap, the administrator was able to hit the ground running while Zandile went out to schools and sold her products.

By increasing the value proposition of your business, you make it more attractive to clients. The more clients you have, the greater will be your ability to employ the people you need to help you grow your business. And when you finally do employ them, delegate effectively and get on with doing what you are meant to be doing – growing your business!

Letting go

At 27, I was marketing director of a business, with about 40 people reporting directly to me. I had crossed the first entrepreneurial hurdle; I was no longer a one-man business. There was a constant queue outside my office. On good days, three people were waiting to see me in the eternal queue; sometimes eight people were waiting to discuss something with me, have me sign something or ask me if they could have a day off.

One day Brett, a 44-year-old man who was the head of research and development, spent half an hour outside my office waiting to see me. When his turn finally came, he asked me to sign a requisition form to buy special screws from a new supplier. The total cost of the screws was R7. I asked him what the screws were for, and, as I posed the question, I had an out-of-body experience. As he stood waiting for my signature, I literally watched myself ask this man, almost double my age, why he needed to spend R7! I thought about the time he had just wasted, and about the time I was spending giving him permission to spend R7. At that moment, I grasped the absurdity of my need to control.

My need for control, my need to feel important, to feel 'in charge' dissipated. I understood that to make money, I would have to let go of my ego. I would have to let go of the need to make myself important by keeping those around me small. Brett's having to get my signature, my approval as it were, was nothing more than my need for the confirmation that 'I'm important. This is my business and I'm in charge'.

Human beings need ego strokes. We need to be liked and we like to be needed. Perhaps entrepreneurs need even more ego-stroking than most. After all, it takes some kind of ego to go out on your own, to say, 'I have something unique, different or better, to offer the world'. So entrepreneurs start their businesses, and the lucky or skilled ones begin to succeed. Suddenly, they need to employ someone else. But the business is growing and they don't have much time to select and screen the candidate properly; they give him a quick orientation, if there's time, and throw the new employee into the business. Before long, the hapless employee is at the entrepreneur's office door, needing to ask a question, to have a document signed or because there's a problem with a client. It doesn't take long before the entrepreneur is irritated – and the employee demoralised.

After the employee has resigned, or been asked to leave, the entrepreneur sits back to reflect: 'If you want something done properly, you must do it yourself,' he muses. The entrepreneur has had his beliefs about his business, and his importance in it, reinforced. Entrepreneurs want things to be done their way. And we believe firmly that only we can do it properly. We create a situation where only we can make decisions. And then we wonder why the people we have employed to grow the business are simply not adding the value we expect from them.

Ego is one of the biggest killers of small businesses. When entrepreneurs make ego-based decisions, rather than business-based decisions, they impede growth and keep their businesses small. Our employees cannot deliver because we set them up to fail. And when they fail, we subconsciously feel important. A cursory glance at the life stories of entrepreneurs reveals that the most successful ones are those smart enough to hire people smarter than themselves. They choose people to do a job and do it well, not to bolster their self-esteem. These entrepreneurs are growth driven, not ego driven. They select people to whom they are able to delegate fully, safe in the knowledge that the employee's success is the business's success.

I have two friends, Larry and Jenny, who are writers. Both work for themselves and take on as much freelance work as they can handle. They are both dedicated to their craft, work hard, and are hoping to strike it rich with a best-seller. In the meantime, they write children's books for a publisher who pays them well. After writing first drafts they both send their work to an editor. The editor's role is to comment critically on their writing. She corrects mistakes, changes words, makes suggestions and checks references. She then sends her comments back to the writer who works on a second draft. This process can be repeated four or five times before a final draft is sent to the publisher for acceptance.

During the editing process, the differences between Larry and Jenny become clear. Larry and the editor fight endlessly. They haggle over words, they argue about references, and every change that the editor

137

makes becomes a negotiation. When Jenny sends her first draft to the editor, she lets it go. The editor can make whatever changes she deems fit. Occasionally they disagree but, for the most part, Jenny allows the editor to do what she does best – edit. Larry needs to control his book. He needs to control the process and he needs to feel in charge. Every change is an insult, every suggestion a rebuke. Jenny, on the other hand, sees herself merely as the catalyst for the book. It is her book in as much as she has written it. But it does not define her! She is happy for the editor to add her expertise. Jenny has learned to delegate effectively. Larry has learned nothing.

Kahlil Gibran, the famous Lebanese-American author, wrote:

> *Your children are not your children.*
> *They come through you but not from you,*
> *And though they are with you, yet they belong not*
> *to you.*

Strange as it may seem, this is how I feel about Raizcorp. I created Raizcorp, it is my business, but it does not belong to me.

What does this have to do with delegation? When I hire a person to work for me, his ability to succeed is directly connected to my ability to allow him to succeed. If I, like Larry, am holding tightly to my vision, to my picture of the book or, in my case, the business, my employee's contributions will be of little value. The editor has stopped working hard on Larry's books. There's no point. Jenny, who doesn't see herself as the owner of the words but rather the vehicle through which they come, ends up with better-selling books than Larry – not because she is a better writer but because she has the ability to delegate that which she is not good at to someone who is better than herself, in this case, at editing for commercial consumption.

Every employee to whom I have delegated a function has as much value to add to the business as I do. My ego and my need to control take second place. This does not mean I don't have an ego. My wife and colleagues will vouch for the fact that my ego is indeed alive and kicking! But whenever I feel the need to challenge a partner or an employee's decision, I first ask myself: 'Am I making an ego decision or a business decision?' If the answer is the latter, I intervene; if, however, I am making an ego decision, I quietly let the employee get on with the job he has been given to do.

Many entrepreneurs struggle with this. Many business owners reject an employee's idea, not on the basis of the idea's merit, but simply because the idea did not come from the 'boss'. They allow their ego to take precedence and the business stays stuck – a one-man band fulfilling the lifestyle entrepreneur's vision, stroking his ego but never expanding, never becoming the successful business that it should be.

The key to successful delegation lies in defining very clearly the roles, not the people, needed in your business. Before we hire anyone at Raizcorp, we make very sure that we understand exactly the role we expect that person to play. When entrepreneurs start a business, they are literally, to use an old expression, 'chief cook and bottle-washer'. As time passes, it becomes necessary to employ someone to wash the bottles. Before you hire the 'bottle-washer', make sure you know exactly what role you expect him to play in your business.

At Raizcorp, we have a role description for every single function needed in the organisation. Sometimes, these role descriptions are very rudimentary. In fact, many of the role descriptions were prepared long before Raizcorp had the money, or the means, to employ people to fill them. From the very beginning of Raizcorp's history, I have written down role descriptions for all the people needed to fulfil my vision. In that way, when the time is right, and the person arrives to fill that role, I have absolute faith that I have found the right person. And that person, in turn, is confidently able to start working immediately. Of course, over time, roles evolve and you have to re-visit them. This is the ongoing process of what Michael E. Gerber calls 'working *on* your business, rather than working *in* your business'.[vi]

PART 7

Getting out there

Networking

While sales are an integral part of growing a business, I don't intend to go into the topic here. There are many books on sales techniques that you can read. I don't profess to be a sales specialist, but I read as much as I can on the subject because without sales, you will not have a business. But people are always asking me how they can meet new people in order to sell their product or service. Many business interactions are born out of individuals meeting in a social, non-business environment, at a wedding or a dinner party perhaps. I know two entrepreneurs who met their 'opportunity' on an aeroplane.

So often, 'networking' is just a line item on the business plan, a part of the entrepreneur's list of sales and marketing activities. Yet, in my opinion, it is one of the crucial differentiators of successful entrepreneurs. Entrepreneurs who network understand that networking is not about selling. Networking is about being interested in other people. Having an interest in the people around you is an important part of being a successful entrepreneur. In this section, I will provide some pointers to help you become a more skilled networker.

Be sincere

Successful entrepreneurs enjoy their journey. I believe that there is a direct correlation between how much you enjoy what you do and the success you achieve in doing it.

When you are networking, make sure you are connecting with people that you like. If you meet someone, and you get a sense that you do not like the person, politely end the conversation and walk away – even if that person happens to be the director of a large company that might give you business. Trust your gut and don't pursue the relationship.

Sincerity is the most fundamental aspect of effective networking. A relationship established in a networking environment, without sincerity, will not last.

If you focus on the ultimate aim of making money, and not on enjoying the people you meet along the way – and learning and growing from that interaction – your approach has no integrity, and chances are that you will not achieve the success you desire. Developing successful relationships is an essential element of being an entrepreneur.

No one is unimportant

Be humble and remember that no one is unimportant. Speak to everyone as if that person is the most important person in the room. Homing in on one particular person at a networking event, knowing that the individual is a managing director or the like, and ignoring all others, is a ticket to failure. In networking, everyone is important. The secretary you ignore in favour of someone you perceive to be more important may be married to someone who could benefit your cause immensely. That secretary may be the person who helps you get an otherwise elusive appointment.

Learn more than you teach

As entrepreneurs, we are so passionate about what we do that, given the chance to tell people about it, we will go on for hours. But not many people are that interested. Some people advise us to be passionate, and show that passion at every opportunity. My advice is to keep your passion bridled, so that when you share it with others, you do not come across as overbearing; you don't dominate the conversation. Talk less; listen more. Rather learn more by asking questions. Remember – and acknowledge – that the other person is important. By asking questions, you place yourself in the position of being able to identify opportunities. If you are the one doing all the talking, you will never be in a position to listen, and to spot opportunities in what you are hearing. By listening and asking questions, you expose yourself to the potential opportunity. This is one of the most difficult things I will ask of you. Keeping quiet, when you are passionate about your business and have spent so much time and effort building it, is no easy feat. When people casually ask what we do, we tend to enthusiastically present a synopsis of our business, telling the unsuspecting person practically every detail about it. This is why the elevator pitch is so important. By keeping your answer subtle and succinct, you allow yourself the opportunity to learn from these meetings, rather than simply to teach.

Networking is not about selling; it is about listening and learning. By launching into a lengthy explanation, you are trying to sell. This is not the appropriate environment for the hard sell. The time for selling your business is in a business environment. Networking is not that environment. Networking is informal; business meetings are not. Unless the person specifically asks for more detail, don't volunteer it.

Have your elevator pitch prepared

You need to have your elevator pitch ready at all times. It needs to come out automatically. You cannot be ambiguous or hesitant. The pitch must be a concise, exciting and enticing explanation of what it is that you do. In order to explain your business in a few seconds, every word must be considered, but your delivery must be spontaneous. For this reason, you must practise the pitch, without sounding unnatural. An effective pitch will attract the attention of the listener and make him want to ask questions to find out more.

Sign up!

When companies join Raizcorp, I try to find out what interests and hobbies the entrepreneur has. Wine and golf are two interests that classically fit this bill. I then suggest that the entrepreneur joins a wine-tasting club or a golf club, or any organisation where he can meet people, in order to network with them. This provides an effective way to meet people in a non-business environment. You can get to know them, and they can get to know you. You can expose what you do to the people you encounter. The point is to expose yourself to new circles of people from a certain target market, or of a particular calibre. By joining an organisation, such as a wine-tasting club, you and your fellow members already have something in common. This often presents you with the requisite 'ice-breaker', in much the same way that a shared interest in a sport might provide. Many successful partnerships have started over a casual discussion about the weekend's football game. This immediately sets up a rapport. By getting to know people in a non-business environment, you get to see them with their guard down.

You also need to join clubs and associations that are specifically related to your product or service. While events such as conferences that relate specifically to your product or service obviously present a great opportunity to network, this type of networking is far more important in terms of keeping abreast with developments in your particular industry and keeping a profile within the industry, than an opportunity to meet new people and potential customers.

Subscribe

When you meet people, you will find out that they are interested in certain things, such as whisky or cooking. A great way to show a person that you are interested in them is to send them information that is unrelated to business. People like to surround themselves with the things they like or in which they are interested. A person's office often provides several clues about their likes or hobbies. Anyone walking into my office will know that I like whisky and movies. Casual conversation is another great indicator of people's likes and interests. For example, on meeting someone and finding out that they are interested in whisky, spend some time looking for an interesting (preferably obscure) site on the Internet that relates to whisky, and send the person the details, mentioning that you thought the site might interest them. By doing this, you create a contact point with the individual, expand your own horizons and make an excellent impression on your new acquaintance. This might sound contrived, but it is a strategic move aimed at finding and maximising commonalities with new people who come into your world. By taking these steps, you give the person the message that you have thought about them, and this message is almost always well-received. If business comes from the association, then well and good. But even if no business comes from it, it doesn't matter. As I've mentioned before, networking is not just about making new business contacts. It is about being interested in other people. Communicate with people because they interest you. If business comes from it, that's a bonus.

Get your life partner involved

If networking is your aim, you can quite easily find yourself in a networking environment every night of the week. If you have a life partner, this can become very taxing on your relationship. By excluding your partner from these events, you create more pressure at home, which may lead to the relationship ending or force you to stay at home more, thereby missing potentially vital networking opportunities. Encourage your partner to accompany you to these functions. Their participation will prevent them from feeling excluded. In addition, people like to see people with partners. It creates the impression of stability and support. Your partner confirms to others that your life does not only revolve around business. This puts others at ease, particularly in an informal social environment.

Have fun!

I was recently introduced to a young entrepreneur. When I asked him how things were going, he replied, 'I'm still having fun'.

Having fun is about learning, discovering and being exposed to new and interesting things. Having fun doesn't mean that there aren't moments of pain or anxiety. When it comes to networking, if you're not having fun in that environment, go home! If networking is boring or mundane, then you will achieve nothing constructive. Networking for the sake of networking produces nothing. This is true for every aspect of networking, from integrity to including your life partner.

Always follow up

Networking becomes selling when someone you meet expresses enthusiasm about your business and asks you to contact them with additional information. I am astounded by how many people simply don't bother to follow up when the opportunity is handed to them. Perhaps, through inefficiency, laziness or fear, they just don't bother to contact the interested party, and the opportunity is lost. Always follow up. If you say you'll do it, do it!

The hidden power of business cards

I hate to see an entrepreneur meeting someone who expresses interest in their business, but when asked for a business card says they do not have a card with them. The opportunity is lost. Whenever you give someone your card, ask for their card as well. Always have your business card on you, and have your spouse or partner keep a couple just in case, so that when opportunity does knock, you can always do something about it.

How many business cards have you handed out or collected in the past year? And, what did you do with those cards? People consider business cards to be a vitally important part of the networking process, yet pay little attention to what is on them or to what actually needs to be on them. Business cards can provide an incredible amount of information about people and their position in the organisation where they work. But you need to know how to read the business card so that you are able to open up the conversation and start to 'unpack' the person based on the information, or lack thereof, on the card. I want to share some secrets on the way I 'read' business cards.

The first thing I do is feel the card. Corporate business cards are usually printed on thicker paper. The thicker the card, the more the business prides itself on its image in the market place. Generally, 'fly-by-night' operators will not use thick, expensive or textured paper.

Another quick way to see whether you are dealing with a 'fly-by-night' operator, as opposed to a serious business, is to look at both the print quality and cut of the card. Many people approach me with business cards that they have made on their computer, printed at home and then cut out themselves to save costs. It is very difficult to do this perfectly. Home-made cards, cut skew, tell you that the entrepreneur does not have enough money to have his cards professionally produced. Poor print quality is an indicator that the card was done on a home printer. The use of icons from your computer is also a give-away that the card was designed on your home computer. And, whatever you do, don't put 'clip art' on your business cards! Handing out home-made business cards sends the message that you are either cash-strapped or not serious about your business. Remember that, as much as you are judging others' cards, they are judging yours!

There are other tell-tale signs on a business card. For example, when the fax and telephone number are the same, it's likely that the business is a small operation. If they are the same, rather just supply the phone number and let people phone you for the fax number. The other big giveaway is the e-mail address. Is the domain name a normal ISP (e.g. @yahoo) or is it the company's name? Can the business afford its own domain? Make the investment and get a domain in your company's name. It sends a message of credibility and professionalism – and perception is all-important in the entrepreneurial world!

When a businessman in Japan receives a business card, he takes it with both his hands, looks at it carefully and reads the information out loud. He then puts the card on the table in front of him or even into a special cardholder. This ritual is known as *meishi kokan*. Business cards are not merely taken and slipped into pockets or wallets. The exchange of business cards expresses that the two people value each other and appreciate the opportunity to meet. There are great lessons in *meishi kokan*.

From now on, when you receive a business card, take the time to absorb the information on it. Remember, as the Japanese do, that the person's name is on the business card – you need to take cognisance of that, and respect that. Take the card into your hand, or even both hands, and look at it carefully because it is going to be your biggest ally in 'unpacking' the person who has handed it to you.

Firstly, it is going to allow you to remember the person's name – there is nothing worse than forgetting someone's name when you are going into a meeting with them, especially when it's a potential client. Secondly, it allows you to find out more about the business. The name of the business is very important. Generally, people give their business a name that means something important to them, such as their children's names, or a combination of their name and their partner's name. Asking the person what the name of their business means, or where it came from, encourages them to tell you a little bit more about the business.

In my case, there's a story behind the name Raizcorp. Obviously, Raiz is my surname. But 'corp'? What has 'corp' got to do with entrepreneurs? There's a long story as to how that came about. If somebody had to ask me about the name, I would be forced to tell them the story, which would then tell them a whole lot of things about me. They would learn from the story that I play social poker; they would learn that I'm interested in public speaking or in people who speak in public; they would learn that I'm interested in technology. In short, by asking me where the name Raizcorp comes from, they would learn things about me that I would not reveal in the normal course of conversation.

Another way to explore a business card is to ask about the logo. What does it mean? Why did the person choose it? When you start to analyse the card, a person might say, for example, 'I'm interested in astronomy and that's why I have stars in my logo; it's also about reaching for the stars'. Now you know that the person has ambition and is interested in astronomy. You could ask him if he's been to the planetarium or whether he has a telescope. And, suddenly, you're connecting. You're engaging with the person on his level, on a topic of interest to him. And, once people are talking about things that are dear to them, they warm up, and the barriers come down.

The other obvious place to look is at the person's job title. If it's vague, or something you haven't heard of, you could ask the person what it really means. You could also ask them how long they've been in the position and that could lead to your asking them what work they did previously.

By slowly finding out a bit of the person's history and looking for things that you may have in common, or people that you may both know, you begin to form a connection with that person.

The ubiquitous business card has the potential, if used properly, to reveal vital information about its owner that may lead to a better understanding, and help you to find common ground between you. Now that you have made the connection, it's about proving your value proposition, making the sale, supplying your product or service – and collecting the cash!

Conclusion

It struck me while writing this book, that many of my life's greatest moments, decisions and realisations have taken place near the sea. Running on the beachfront, I came across the fast-food wrappers that led to my first business. While watching the waves in Durban, I made a very personal and difficult decision to leave the family business to pursue my own path. And, most significantly, I conceived Raizcorp while sitting on a patio overlooking the Umhlanga beach. Even now, while I live in Johannesburg, whenever I need to make big changes or engage in serious long-term planning, I try to take myself to a beach. I sit on the sand, notebook in hand, and find that inspiration comes more easily when I have the horizon of the ocean to keep me focused.

Since having children, I have also spent time on the beach building sandcastles, an activity I hadn't done for a long time. I recently found myself mesmerised, watching my oldest son building a sandcastle. I observed him looking for the right spot, surveying the other children's castles and, finally, begining his building task. I couldn't help but start to think of the many similarities between what he was doing and what I, and the many entrepreneurs with whom I work, do on a daily basis.

The first thing the boy had to do was find the right location for his sandcastle. Of course, the biggest decision regarding where to locate a sandcastle has to do with the tides, and he is too young to understand that concept. As it happened, on this particular occasion we arrived at the beach as the tide was coming in. This did not deter him. Instinctively he knew that, if he waited for everything to be perfect, he would never begin. Unlike many entrepreneurs – who are waiting for the perfect moment before they begin – my son just began building. I watched as he looked around to see where the other children were locating their sandcastles. And, then, he found a spot not too far from the others, but with enough distance to give him both the space and the right type of sand: sand that is too dry would crumble while sand that is too wet would not hold.

Like building a sandcastle, starting a business is a combination of finding the correct location and having the right resources with which to build the business. Not unlike the boy on the beach, entrepreneurs need to observe their competition; they need to know what is happening in the markets; and they need to fully survey the 'scene' of their market place before they begin their building process. There is nothing simple about building a sandcastle. Like a business, a good sandcastle requires planning and patience. There is an equal mix of art and science. It's messy, unpredictable and subject to the wind and the waves, with the builder never having complete control over his end-product. The builder's role is to keep going and keep building. Most importantly, he needs to keep reading the signals and signs coming from the environment around him, until the desired end is reached.

Of course, no amount of planning will substitute for getting started. Having found the desired location, the actual building of the sandcastle begins – it is a slow process that requires methodical building, packing and repacking. There is no correct way to build a sandcastle. Some builders begin with a huge mound of sand and chip away at it as they sculpt. For me, these builders are the 'big idea' entrepreneurs. They have a grandiose plan, and building their business requires them to, slowly and methodically, refine the idea until they have built their castle. Other builders start at the bottom. There are those who build the foundation slowly but widely. Once they have created a strong foundation, they begin to build – with a good chance of building a very high sandcastle. Others start by building a smaller foundation. Once they have built to the maximum capacity, they return to the foundation and reinforce it. I have seen all three types of entrepreneurs. There are those who chip away, there are those who go high quickly – and then return to the base. My own experience at Raizcorp has been to build a very broad foundation – slowly and methodically, over years. And, now that the foundation is well established, we are building a tall castle with many rooms and high towers.

However one chooses to build, sandcastles require a lot of careful patting. I like to call this 'the art of the pat' – it is a key aspect of building both a successful business and a sturdy sandcastle. If you pat too hard, the castle falls; if you pat too softly, nothing sticks. And then, patting too hard on one side may cause damage on the other. Learning to apply just the right degree of pressure is something that only the experience itself can render.

As the tide started to slowly come in, and small waves began to endanger the base of the castle, my son began to reinforce the base with additional sand.

Some builders choose to build a wall to protect their castle, others create a moat. There are a myriad factors conspiring against success – only the builder's careful planning and persistence stand between a mighty sandcastle and a heap of sand.

And even when the sandcastle seems nearly complete, the builder cannot rest. Watching my son patting away at the one side of his castle, I realised that the other side of his castle was about to crumble. In my mind, this would be disastrous. I kept silent though, more interested in his response than in saving his sandcastle. To my surprise, he was almost oblivious to the fact that his sandcastle was about to collapse. As a huge chunk of sand fell away, he simply picked up the sand and kept going. I think he saw the falling down merely as part of the process of building a castle. He did not perceive the 'near-disaster' as a problem – it was simply something that happens when you build a castle. As entrepreneurs, there are many such 'mini-collapses' on the way to success – a major client leaves, a devoted staff member emigrates, markets take a downturn. The builder's response to these events is all-important. Just then, another child threw a tantrum as his sandcastle began to crumble. I wondered if these different responses are innate or taught.

The height of the castle is really a function of the builder's desire. What he thinks is possible, based on a combination of his previous experience as well as the castles around him, will – to a large degree – determine his success. My son was not intimidated by the older children whose castles were rising more rapidly than his; rather, the competition seemed to spur him on. At times, he reached for a bucket, and, at one point, he called his younger brother to help him. Being able to make use of the resources that surround an entrepreneur are key to the success of the business. At this point, I was so inspired by his determination that, had he asked, I would gladly have assisted him. Successful entrepreneurs are able to inspire those around them. As he began to reach the end of his building, I realised that my son had taught me valuable lessons about entrepreneurship and what it takes to build a successful business. The teacher had become the pupil.

While there is as much reward in the creation as there is in the completion of the structure, there comes a point when the builder can indeed step back and admire his creation. Looking at the result, he will hopefully be satisfied with his handiwork. He may see places where he could have done something differently; he may see kinks he never realised were there. Ideally, the builder is able to look at his creation with pride: He has built something from nothing. His persistence, patience and imagination have realised the creation of a thing of beauty.

And then, like all the products of our persistence and imagination, there comes a time when the builder must leave his creation behind. There is nothing permanent about a sandcastle. In fact, it is the transient nature of the creation that makes its building all the more precious. Overnight, the tide will rise and the waves will destroy the structure. The next day, when a child comes to the beach, he won't know anything about the sandcastle that stood there the day before. Should he choose to build a sandcastle of his own, the builders who came before will have tips for him – they will have learned from their experience and will be able to guide the new builder. He, however, will have to find his own way of building his sandcastle.

In his book, *Good to Great*,[vii] Jim Collins describes great businesses as those that are built by leaders who are consistent, who build their 'sandcastles' methodically, from the bottom up, who put in place the correct processes and the right management team (neither too 'wet' nor too 'dry'). They are the builders whose ambition matches their work ethic. Ultimately, that is what the successful entrepreneurial business comes down to – a lot of desire, which is matched by an equal amount of hard work.

I trust, as you come to the end of this book, that you have what it takes to build your sandcastle, methodically and with passion. Know this: building your castle is messy and sometimes unpredictable, but when you step back and look at it, after years of building and continual patting, you will experience such a feeling of pride that the journey will have been worth it. As you build, I wish you sunshine, good quality sand and, above all, a robust sandcastle that will withstand whatever waves come your way.

References

i   Graves, William D. 1994. *The Portable MBA in Entrepreneurship.* John Wiley & Sons. http://www.extension.iastate.edu/agdm

ii   http://www.cyberindian.com/mother-teresa/mother-teresa-my-marketing-hero.php

iii   http://www.achieving-life-abundance.com/visualization.html

iv   http://www.wordnet.princeton.edu/perl/webwn

v   Wagner, Rodd and Gale Muller. 2009. *The Power of 2, How to Make the Most of Your Partnerships at Work and in Life.* Gallup Press

vi   Gerber Michael E. 1995. *The E-myth revisited: why most small businesses don't work and what to do about it.* Harper Business

vii   Collins Jim. 2001. *Good to Great: Why Some Companies Make the Leap... and Others Don't.* Harper Business